Science Projects
About Light

Science Projects
About Light

Robert Gardner

● Science Projects ●

ENSLOW PUBLISHERS, INC.

44 Fadem Road	P.O. Box 38
Box 699	Aldershot
Springfield, N.J. 07081	Hants GU12 6BP
U.S.A.	U.K.

Library of Congress Cataloging-in-Publication Data

Gardner, Robert, 1929-
  Science projects about light / Robert Gardner.
      p.   cm. — (Science projects)
  Includes bibliographic references and index.
  ISBN 0-89490-529-5
  1. Light—Experiments—Juvenile literature. 2. Science
projects—Juvenile literature. 3. Science—Exhibitions—
Juvenile literature.
  [1. Light—Experiments. 2. Experiments. 3. Science projects.]
  I. Title. II. Series: Gardner, Robert, 1929- Science projects.
QC360.G39 1994
535'.078—dc20   93-23719
                                                                      CIP
                                                                       AC
Printed in the United States of America

10 9 8 7 6 5 4 3

Illustration Credits: Stephen F. Delisle

Cover Photo: Stuart Simons, 1994

Contents

*appropriate for science fair project ideas

*appropriate for science fair project ideas

Introduction

This book is filled with science projects and experiments about light. Most of the materials you will need to carry out these activities can be found in your home or school. Some of the experiments may require materials that you can buy in a supermarket, a hobby shop, or a hardware store. You will need someone to help you with a few activities that require more than one pair of hands and, if any danger is involved, it will be indicated. It would be best if you work with friends or adults who enjoy experimenting as much as you do. In that way you will all enjoy what you are doing.

Like a good scientist, you will find it useful to record your ideas, notes, data, and anything you can conclude from your experiments in a notebook. By so doing, you can keep track of the information you gather and the conclusions you reach. It will allow you to refer back to other experiments you have done that may be useful to you in projects you will do later.

Science Fairs

Some of the projects in this book may be appropriate for a science fair. Those projects are indicated with an asterisk (*). However, judges at such fairs do not reward projects or experiments that are simply copied from a book. For example, a model of the human eye, which is commonly found at these fairs, would probably not impress judges unless it was done in a novel or creative way. A model of the eye with a flexible lens that could produce images of objects at any distance from the "eye" would receive more consideration than a rigid papier-mâché model.

Science fair judges tend to reward creative thought and imagination. It is difficult to be creative or imaginative unless you are really interested in your project, so choose something that appeals to you. Before you jump into a project, consider, too, your own talents and the cost of materials you will need.

If you decide to use a project found in this book for a science fair, you should find ways to modify or extend the project. This should not be difficult because you will probably discover that, as you do these projects, new ideas for experiments will come to mind. These new experiments could make excellent science fair projects, particularly because the ideas are your own and are interesting to you.

If you decide to enter a science fair and have never done so before, you should read some of the books listed in the bibliography. The references that deal specifically with science fairs will provide plenty of helpful hints and lots of useful information that will enable you to avoid the pitfalls that sometimes plague first-time entrants. You will learn how to prepare appealing reports that include charts and graphs, how to set up and display your work, how to present your project, and how to relate to judges and visitors.

Safety First

Most of the projects included in this book are perfectly safe. However, the following safety rules are well worth reading before you start any project.

1. Do any experiments or projects, whether from this book or of your own design, under the supervision of a science teacher or other knowledgeable adult.

2. Read all instructions carefully before proceeding with a project. If you have questions, check with your supervisor before going any further.

3. Maintain a serious attitude while conducting experiments. Fooling around can be dangerous to you and to others.

4. Wear approved safety goggles when you are doing anything that might cause injury to your eyes.

5. Do not eat or drink while experimenting.

6. Have a first aid kit nearby while you are experimenting.

7. Do not put your fingers or any object other than properly designed electrical connectors into electrical outlets.

8. Never experiment with household electricity except under the supervision of a knowledgeable adult.

9. Do not touch a light bulb. Light bulbs produce light, but they also produce heat.

10. Never look directly at the sun. It can cause permanent damage to your eyes.

1

Paths of Light

A surveyor looking through a transit or an artist establishing perspec-
tive for a painting both assume that light travels in straight lines.
Scientists also make assumptions about light, but they try to prove or
demonstrate that their assumptions are correct. In this chapter, you
will do some experiments to determine whether or not light travels in
straight lines. Then you will investigate ways to change the paths
followed by light.

1.1 Does Light Travel In Straight Lines?*

Assuming that light travels in straight lines does not mean that it actually does. Here is a way to check this assumption. Use clear plastic tape to fasten a small piece of colored cellophane to a window.

Things you'll need:

- small piece of colored cellophane
- window where lots of light enters
- clear plastic tape
- long mailing tubes

The fact that you can see the cellophane does not prove light follows a straight-line path from the window to your eye. To restrict the paths that light might follow in traveling from the cellophane to your eye, hold one end of a long, narrow mailing tube close to the colored cellophane. Look through the other end of the tube. Can you see the cellophane? **Don't look at the sun!** It can damage your eyes.

Now make a straight tube as long as possible by taping several mailing tubes together. (You may need a long, straight stick to support the tubes.) Have a friend hold one end of the tube near the cellophane while you look through the other end. Can you still see the cellophane? Do the results of this experiment help confirm the assumption that light travels in straight lines?

- What can you do to show that light travels in straight lines over longer distances than you have measured so far?

- What other experiments can you do to test the idea that light travels in straight lines?

1.2 Pinhole Images and Light Paths*

Here is another way to test the idea that light travels in straight lines. Look closely at the drawing in Figure 1a. It shows light rays (very narrow beams of light) coming from a bright object. If these straight lines of light pass through a tiny hole, they should produce an upside down image of the object on a screen beyond the pinhole. In this experiment, you will check to see if such an image can be produced. If it can, it offers more evidence that light travels in straight lines. Furthermore, as you can see from the drawing, if the screen is as far from the pinhole as the object from which the light comes, then the image and object should be the same size.

Things you'll need:

- cardboard box
- candle and candle holder
- scissors
- black construction paper
- ruler
- large straight pin, such as a T-pin or hat pin
- dark room
- sheet of white cardboard or sheet of white paper taped to cardboard
- light socket or lamp
- clear light bulb with straight-line filament
- pencil
- an adult to help you

Ask an adult to help you with this experiment. Place a box near a candle as shown in Figure 1b. Cut a hole about an inch square in the box and cover it with a sheet of black construction paper. Using a ruler, measure the height of the tip of the candle's wick. Then use a large pin, such as a T-pin or hat pin, to make a small hole in the black paper at the same height as the tip of the wick.

Ask the adult to help you light the candle. Then turn out all the lights so that the room is completely dark except for the candle light. Hold a sheet of white cardboard or paper taped to cardboard near the opposite side of the box. Can you find the candle's image on the cardboard screen? Is it upside down? How does the size of the image

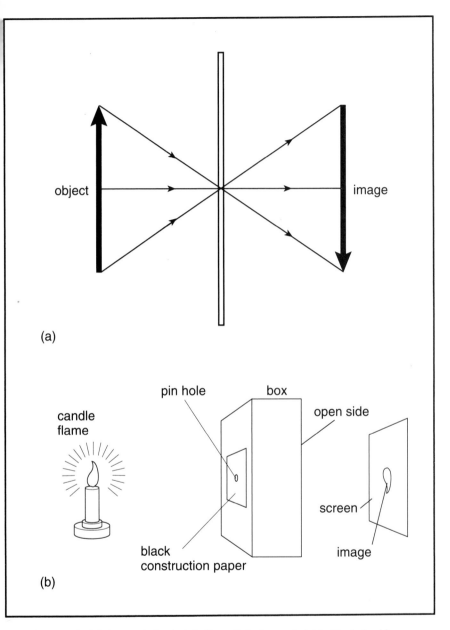

(a)

(b)

Figure 1-a) If light travels in straight lines, light from a bright object should pass through a pinhole to form an inverted image on a screen. 1-b) This idea can be tested with a candle, a pinhole, and a screen.

change as you move the screen closer to the pinhole? Farther from the pinhole? How does the drawing in Figure 1a help you explain why the size of the image changes?

Replace the candle with a clear light bulb that has a straight-line filament. (See Figure 2.) Turn the bulb so that the full length of its filament faces the pinhole. (Your adult helper may have to adjust the socket or lamp to make this possible.) Can you obtain a pinhole image using the light bulb's filament?

Can you tell whether the image of the filament is upside down or right side up? If not, slowly move a pencil up and down in front of the bulb as you watch the image. How does this help you determine whether the image is inverted or not? How can you use the pencil to determine whether the image is reversed left to right? Is the image reversed vertically? Is it reversed horizontally?

Place the screen and filament so they are both the same distance from the pinhole. Does the length of the image appear to be about the same as the length of the filament? What would you have to do to test this more closely?

How have the results of these experiments helped you determine whether light travels in straight lines?

- On a bright sunny day, look at the circles of light (sun dapples) that appear in the shade of a leafy tree. What do you think causes these circles? What experiment could you do to help confirm your explanation (hypothesis)?

- Make a pinhole viewer as shown in Figure 3. Remove both lids from a tin can. Cover one end with tissue or waxed paper. Hold the paper in place with a rubber band. Use a small nail to make a hole through the bottom of an empty box of cereal. Put the can inside the box so that the center of its open end is over the hole in the box. Point the box at something bright such as a light bulb. Do you expect the pinhole image to be right side up or inverted? Were you right? What happens to the size of the image as you move the box

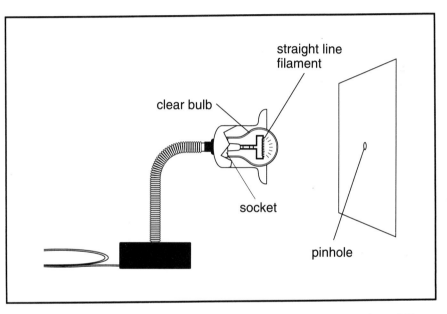

Figure 2) Can a clear bulb with a straight-line filament produce a pinhole image? If it can, how can you tell whether or not it is inverted?

closer to the bright object? Make a diagram to show why this happens.

- If you like photography, you might enjoy building a pinhole camera. Pinhole cameras can be used even in dim light to take photographs of stationary objects. Why can't a pinhole camera be used for action photos? Some suggestions for making a pinhole camera can be found in the book *Experimenting with Light* by Robert Gardner. (See the bibliography at the back of this book.)

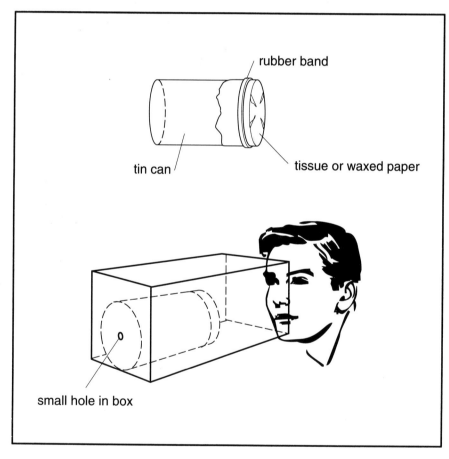

Figure 3) A pinhole viewer.

1.3 Light and Matter

Sunlight passes through the vacuum of space, the air that makes up the atmosphere, and even the solid glass in windows. Substances through which light passes, such as air and glass, are said to be transparent. Can you name some other things that are transparent?

Things you'll need:

- light bulb, lamp and socket
- plastic wrap
- tissue paper
- cardboard

Look at a glowing light bulb through a sheet of plastic wrap. Is the plastic transparent? How can you tell? Now look at the bulb through a sheet of tissue paper. Can you see the bulb clearly? Does light come through the paper?

Substances that transmit light but reflect so much of it in different directions that you cannot see through it are said to be translucent. Can you name some things that are translucent?

Now hold a sheet of cardboard in front of your eyes. Can you see the bulb through the cardboard? Objects that transmit no light are said to be opaque. Name some things that are opaque.

1.4 Light and Shadows*

In an otherwise dark room, turn on a single frosted light bulb. Hold an opaque object—your hand will do—between the light bulb and a thin sheet of cardboard that is within about 12 in. (30 cm) of the bulb. Describe the shadow cast by your hand on the cardboard screen.

Things you'll need:

- frosted light bulb, lamp and socket
- thin sheet of cardboard
- light-colored wall
- tin can

What happens to the shadow as you move your hand closer to the screen? Farther from the screen?

Move the screen several yards (meters) from the light and repeat the experiment. What happens to the shadow as you move your hand closer to the screen? Farther from the screen? What is different when the shadows are on a screen farther from the light?

Place the light bulb at one end of a room opposite a light-colored wall that can serve as a screen. What is the biggest shadow of your hand that you can make on the wall? Where should you hold your hand to do this? What's the smallest shadow of your hand that you can make on the wall? Where should you hold your hand to do this?

Hold a tin can about 20 in. (50 cm) from the wall and turn it in various ways. How many different shadow shapes can you make? Try a number of other objects. What interesting shadow shapes can you make with them?

1.5 Shadows: Sharp and Fuzzy*

Compare the shadows you made in the previous section with the ones you can make using a tensor bulb, which has a very small filament, or a clear bulb with a straight-line filament. If the straight filament is viewed from the end, as shown in Figure 4, it is very nearly a point of light.

Things you'll need:

- materials used in previous experiment
- sunlight
- tensor bulb and lamp or clear bulb with straight-line filament

Use the point of light made by the tensor bulb or the clear bulb and the end of its straight filament to make shadows of your hand on the wall. How do these shadows compare with those made using a frosted bulb? Under what conditions might a frosted bulb produce shadows similar to those made with a point of light?

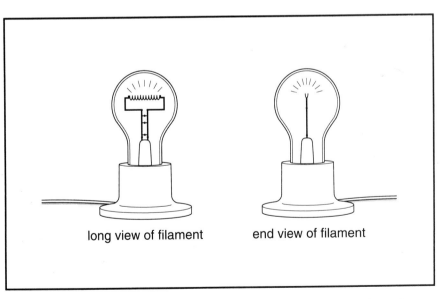

long view of filament   end view of filament

Figure 4) A straight-line filament when viewed from one end is very nearly a point of light.

You've examined shadows made with a point of light and a larger light. How do these shadows suggest that light travels in straight lines?

- What's the smallest shadow of your hand that you can make?

- Using the point of light and your hands see if you can make shadows that resemble the heads of various animals or objects. Can you make a house? A church? A rabbit's head? A dog's? An elephant's?

- All three of the shadows shown in Figure 5 can be made with the same object. Using clay, see if you can make a single object that can cast the shadows shown when turned at various angles to the light. What does the object look like?

- Are the shadows cast in sunlight sharp or fuzzy? Does sunlight, which travels 150,000,000 million kilometers to reach the earth, appear to come from a point source or from a bigger source of light? How do you know? How do shadows cast in sunlight change from sunrise to sunset? Why do you think the shadow of a bird or an airplane is usually fuzzy?

Figure 5) These three shadows were cast by the same object. What does the object look like?

- Do you ever have more than one shadow? If so, what conditions are needed for you to cast more than one shadow? If you were to stand near a street or a porch light on a night when there was a full moon, how many shadows would you have?

Very Large Shadows—Eclipses

Sometimes when the sun, moon, and earth are all in a line, the moon's shadow falls on the earth, causing an eclipse of the sun. As you can see from Figure 6, no sunlight reaches the umbra—the dark part of the moon's shadow. The penumbra, or lighter part of the shadow, is illuminated by some parts of the sun. From Figure 6, see if you can identify the parts of the sun that illuminate the penumbra. If you were in the small region of the Earth touched by the umbra, what would

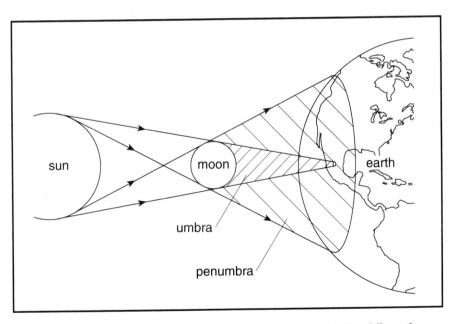

Figure 6) We may see an eclipse of the sun when the moon's shadow falls on the earth's surface. The lines with arrows represent light rays from the sun that form the boundaries of the umbra and penumbra.

happen to the sun during the eclipse? How would the sun appear if you were in the penumbra?

How can the drawing in Figure 6 help you explain the fuzzy shadows cast by objects illuminated by an extended light source such as a frosted bulb or the sun?

- Look at a variety of shadows, including your own, that are cast in sunlight. See if you can explain why some parts of the shadow are sharp and others fuzzy. Look at the shadow of a wire that is close to the ground. Then look at the shadow of an overhead telephone wire. Which shadow is fuzzier? Can you explain why?

- When the planets Mercury and Venus, which are both larger than the moon, pass between the Earth and the sun, we are not aware of any eclipse of the sun. See if you can figure out why. Building a scale model might help.

1.6 Shadows and Time*

Watch your shadow in sunlight during the course of a day. How does it change? When is it longest? When is it shortest? Does the direction in which your shadow points change during the day?

Drive a stake into level ground in an open area that is bathed in sunlight. Use a carpenter's level to be sure the stake is vertical. Watch to see how the shadow of the stake changes during the course of a day. In what direction does the shadow point shortly after sunrise? At midday? Near sunset? When is it longest? Shortest?

Things you'll need:
- yardstick or meter stick
- stake
- level ground in sunlight
- carpenter's level
- cardboard
- pencil
- clock or watch

If you live north of latitude 23.5° (anywhere in the United States except Hawaii), the shadow cast by the stake will point due north at midday. That is when the sun is highest in the sky. Fasten a large, level sheet of cardboard to the ground just north of the stake and watch the shadow closely during the two-hour period around midday. As the stake's shadow grows shorter and shorter, draw it on the cardboard. Continue to do this at ten-minute intervals until the shadow begins to grow longer.

- Place a magnetic compass on the cardboard beside the stake's shortest shadow. Does the compass needle point in the same direction as the shortest shadow? Why might they not point in exactly the same direction?

- The shortest shadow you have drawn is the one cast when the sun was highest in the sky. This time is called midday. Each point on Earth has its own local midday, which may not be at noon. Midday occurs when the sun is due south. Why does the midday shadow point due north?

- How is your shadow affected by the season? To find out, measure your shadow at midday at the beginning of each season. How does the length of your midday shadow change from season to season? When is it longest? Shortest?

- During which season is there a time when your shadow points in a direction that is southwest? Southeast? During which season is it impossible to stand in sunlight and cast a shadow that points due east or due west? Does your shadow ever point due south?

- Make a shadow clock or sundial that will allow you to use shadows to tell time. How accurate is your shadow clock? What limitations does it have? What can you do to improve it?

- See if you can find a way to use shadows to map the sun's path across the sky. **Caution: Never look directly at the sun!** If you succeed, map the sun's path at different times of the year. How does the sun's path across the sky change from season to season?

- Astronomers use a very large unit to measure distance. It is called the light-year; it is equal to the distance that light travels in one year. Light travels at a speed of 186,282 miles (299,792 kilometers) per second in a vacuum. See if you can find out the length of a light-year in miles and kilometers. Then find the distances to some of the closest and farthest stars.

2

Changing Light Paths

You have seen that light travels in straight lines, but that does not mean the path of a light beam cannot be changed. In this chapter, you will find that the direction of a light beam can be changed dramatically. A mirror can turn a light beam completely around; a lens, or even a glass of water, can bend the straight-line paths of light. By changing the direction of light rays, mirrors and lenses can produce images of the objects from which the light comes. Such is the purpose of mirrors, telescopes, microscopes, and cameras.

2.1 Changing the Path of Light—Reflection in a Plane Mirror*

Let a beam of sunlight coming through a window strike a mirror that you hold in your hand. Can you find a shadow of the mirror on the floor or wall? Has the path of the light that strikes the mirror been changed? How do you know? (If there is no sunlight, you can use the light from a single, bright light bulb on the far side of an otherwise dark room.)

Slowly turn the mirror that you hold in your hand. Can you see a patch of light on a wall or ceiling that moves when you turn the mirror? Place your other hand in front of the mirror. You will see that the patch of light on the wall or ceiling disappears. What does this tell you?

Things you'll need:

- sunlight or light bulb and lamp
- two small plane mirrors
- ruler
- black construction paper
- scissors
- white paper
- protractor
- comb
- white index card
- flashlight

As you have seen, when light "bounces" off a mirror, its path changes dramatically. When the path of light is changed by striking a mirror, we say the light has been reflected. Can light be reflected backward? That is, can the path of a light beam be turned around so it travels in the opposite direction from which it came? Use your mirror to find out.

A Closer Look at Reflection

To see more clearly what happens when light strikes a mirror, you can construct a "ray maker." The ray maker will provide a very narrow beam of light, which you can then reflect with a mirror. To begin, cut a rectangle about 6 in. x 4 in. (15 cm x 10 cm) from a sheet of heavy black construction paper. At the middle of one long edge, use scissors to cut a narrow slit (about 1 mm wide) and 3 in. (7 cm) long. Fold the rectangle and set it on a sheet of white paper so that the slit is vertical as shown in Figure 7-a. In an otherwise dark room, let light from a single bulb several meters away pass through the slit. Use a small plane mirror to reflect the narrow light beam. Turn the mirror so that you can see what happens when the light strikes the mirror at different angles. How does the angle at which the light strikes the mirror (angle *a* in Figure 7-b) appear to compare with the angle at which the

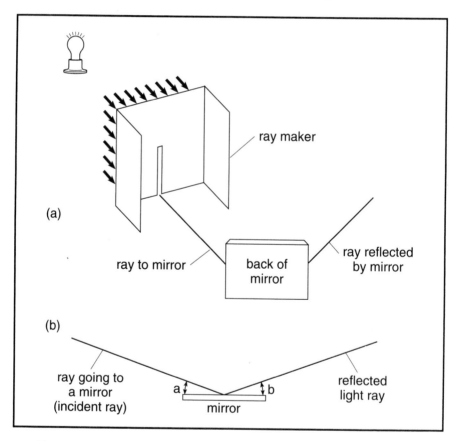

Figure 7-a) A ray maker can be used to produce narrow beams (rays) of light. 7-b) How does angle *a* compare with angle *b* when a light ray is reflected by a mirror?

reflected light leaves the mirror (angle *b* in Figure 7-b)? How can you use a protractor to check your prediction?

To see what happens when a number of narrow, parallel light beams strike the mirror, cut a second rectangle from black construction paper. This time cut a small 2-cm square from the center of one long edge. Fold the rectangle and stand it upright as before several meters from the same light source. Place a comb over the square hole. Light shining through the comb's teeth will make several narrow, nearly parallel beams of light as shown in Figure 8. Do these multiple beams reflect in the same way as a single beam?

Diffuse Reflectors

Repeat the experiment using the ray maker, but replace the mirror with a white index card. What's different when you use the index card in place of the mirror? Look closely. Do you see any evidence that some light is reflected? If so, what's different about this reflected light as compared with the light reflected from a mirror?

Place a sheet of white paper and a sheet of black paper side by side on the floor next to a light-colored wall. Turn off all the lights so that the room is dark. Now, shine a flashlight onto the white paper and then onto the black paper. Look closely at the reflected light you see on the wall as you move the flashlight back and forth between the white and the black paper. How does this experiment indicate that white paper reflects more light than black paper?

If you look into a mirror, you can see your image. Sunlight or artificial light reflected from your body is reflected again by the mirror to produce an image that you can see. Notice that the image of your face appears to be as far behind the mirror as your real face is in front of the mirror. You can see this in another way by holding a ruler perpendicular to the mirror. Notice that the ruler's image appears to extend into the mirror as far as the actual ruler extends outward in front of the mirror.

Hold a piece of white paper in front of your face. You do not see your image because the surface of the white paper is rough; consequently, it reflects light diffusely (in all directions). Because a mirror's surface is very smooth, it reflects any narrow light beam in only one direction, not many. It is the uniform reflection of light from a mirror that enables it to form clear images. You will see how this is done in the next experiment.

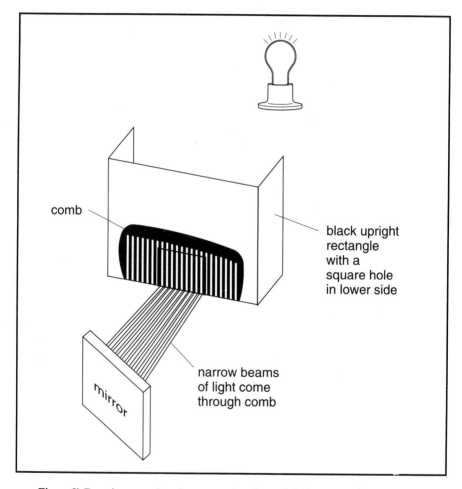

Figure 8) By using a comb and a rectangular piece of black construction paper, you can produce a number of nearly parallel rays of light.

Mirror Images: A Model

From your experiments, you know that light is reflected in an irregular or haphazard way by rough surfaces and in a very uniform way by smooth surfaces such as mirrors. You can make a simple model that will show how mirrors form clear images. To do this, cut a second narrow slit about 1 cm to one side of the slit you made in your ray maker. Place this two-slit ray maker on a long sheet of white paper as shown in Figure 9. Light from a distant light bulb will produce two narrow beams (rays) of light when it passes through the slits in the ray maker.

Have a friend use a mirror to reflect one ray so that the two rays cross. Let the point where the two rays cross represent a point on an object in front of a mirror. Use a second mirror to reflect these two rays as shown in Figure 9. Notice how the two reflected rays diverge. As you can see, these rays appear to come from a point behind the mirror.

Use dotted lines to draw extensions of the two reflected rays back to a point where they appear to meet behind the mirror. Measure the distance from the mirror to the point behind the mirror from where the rays appear to be coming. Is it nearly the same as the distance from the mirror to the point where the rays cross in front of the mirror? How does this model illustrate the way mirrors form images?

Of course, this model is limited. It shows how two light rays from one point on an object are reflected to form just one point on an image that appears to be behind the mirror. With real objects, every point on the object sends out countless rays. But the principle is the same for many points, each with many rays, as it is for one point with two rays. All the rays that strike the mirror from all the many points on the object are reflected to form an image. Rays of light from all points on the object that are reflected by the mirror appear to be coming from behind the mirror. The combination of all these reflected rays produces a clear likeness of the object—an image.

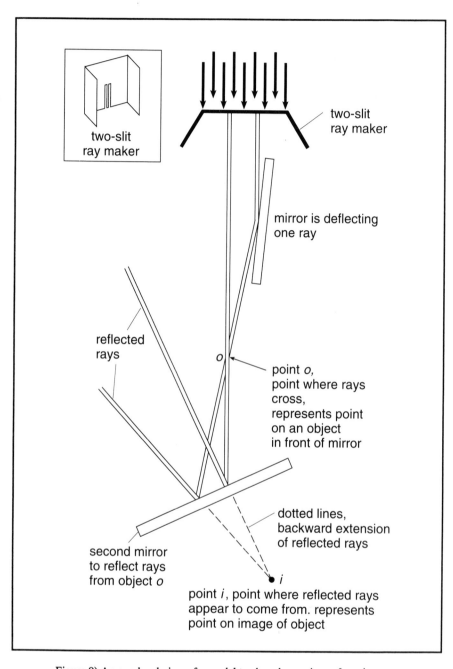

two-slit
ray maker

two-slit
ray maker

mirror is deflecting
one ray

reflected
rays

o

point *o*,
point where rays
cross,
represents point
on an object
in front of mirror

dotted lines,
backward extension
of reflected rays

second mirror
to reflect rays
from object *o*

• *i*

point *i*, point where reflected rays
appear to come from. represents
point on image of object

Figure 9) An overhead view of a model to show how mirrors form images.

Images from Reflected Light

Look at your image in a mirror. Where does your image appear to be? Would you and your image agree on which direction is up? Would you agree about which direction is right? Left?

Use a mirror to read the strange message in Figure 10-a. What does the message say?

Leonardo da Vinci kept notebooks in which he recorded his data, ideas, and conclusions. To keep his notes from being easily read by others, he wrote in such a way that a mirror was required to read his writing. Do you think you could learn to write this way? Do you think Leonardo had to use a mirror to read his notes?

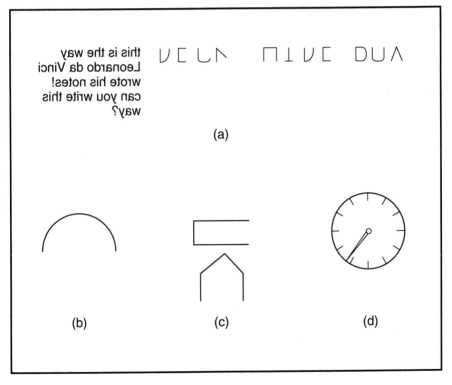

Figure 10) Some mirror puzzlers.

Which of the letters in Figure 10-a appear unchanged when viewed with a mirror? Are there any other letters that would appear unchanged when seen in a mirror? If so, what are they?

How can you use a mirror to make words out of the partial letters found in Figure 10-b? From the incomplete drawings in Figure 10-c, use a mirror to make a complete rectangle of various lengths, a circle, a square, a diamond, and a hexagon. In Figure 10-d, use a mirror to make a clock that reads about 7:13. Can you use the mirror to make a clock that reads exactly 7:20?

• Make some mirror puzzles of your own. Ask your family and friends to solve them.

2.2 *Fun with an Image*

As you have seen, when you look in a mirror, your image appears to be behind the mirror. You can use what you have learned to produce an image that defies reason. **Ask an adult to help you set up this experiment** in a dark room. He or she can light a candle and place it about 6 in. (15 cm) in front of a vertical sheet of window glass. (**To avoid cuts, it would be wise to wear gloves and to tape the edges of the glass.**) Bricks or paperweights can be used to support the glass. Place a large water-filled beaker or jar about 6 in. (15 cm) behind the glass. (See Figure 11.) Move the jar about until the image of the burning candle appears in the center of the jar. If you hide the candle with a metal cookie sheet, you may be able to convince a parent or friend that you have managed to make a candle burn under water.

Things you'll need:
- piece of window glass about 12 inches (30 cm) on a side
- candle and holder
- large water-filled beaker or jar
- tape
- bricks or paperweights
- metal cookie sheet

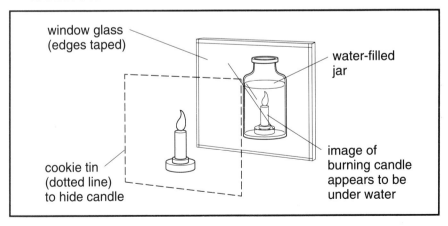

Figure 11) Using the principle of reflection, a candle can be made to appear as if it is burning under water.

2.3 Reflections of Reflections*

Place two plane mirrors at right angles on a sheet of white paper as shown in Figure 12. If necessary, you can use clay to support the mirrors. Use the two-slit ray maker you used in section 2.1 to make two rays of light. Use a third mirror to deflect one ray and intersect the other, making a point of light that represents an "object" between the

Things you'll need:
- three plane mirrors
- clay
- lamp and bulb
- two-slit ray maker
- white paper
- full-length mirror
- hand mirror

mirrors. Notice that the two rays of light coming from the point on the object are reflected twice, once from each mirror. Where would the "images" formed by these reflected rays appear to be? (Of course, other rays, not produced in the model, would go to the second mirror and be reflected as well.)

If you put your finger between the two mirrors, how many images of your finger do you think you will see? Try it. Were you right? Why is there a third image? Can you show that the middle image is due to a double reflection?

What happens to the number of images as you decrease the angle between the mirrors?

Place the two mirrors at right-angles near the edge of a table so you can put your face close to the mirrors. Can you see three images of your face? Wink your right eye. Which eye does the middle image wink? How can you tell that the middle image is due to a double reflection? Are the other two images due to single or double reflections? How can you tell?

Now place the mirrors so that one is horizontal and the other vertical as shown in Figure 13. Place your face near these two mirrors. Why do you think you appear to be upside down in one of the images?

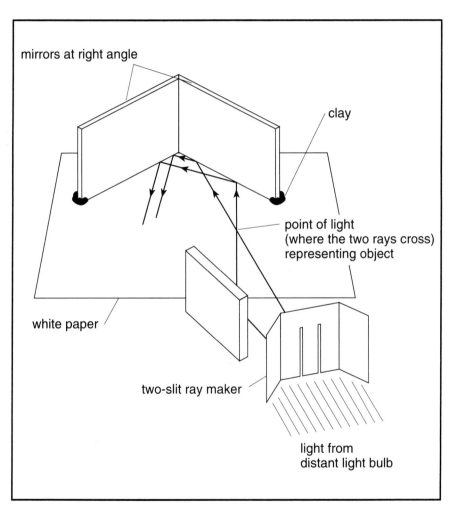

Figure 12) How many images of an object are formed by two mirrors at right angles?

Put your finger between two mirrors whose reflecting surfaces are parallel. Look into one mirror from just above the other one. Carefully adjust the mirrors to see as many images as possible. How many can you see?

Another way to see lots of images is to stand in front of a full-length mirror and hold a large hand mirror just below your eyes with its reflective surface facing the large mirror. Or stand between two large parallel mirrors in a hallway. How many images of yourself

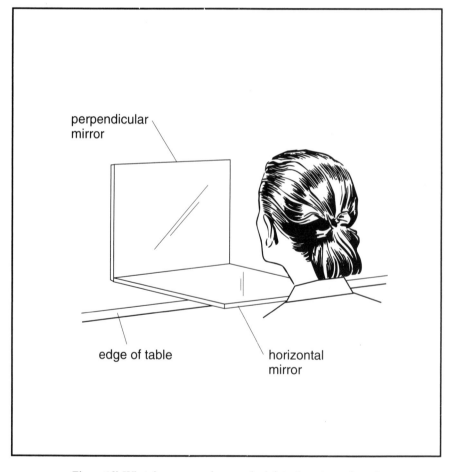

perpendicular mirror

edge of table

horizontal mirror

Figure 13) What do you see when you look into these two mirrors?

can you see? How does the size of the image change with each reflection? Can you explain why?

- Hold two large hand mirrors, one in each hand. Use one mirror to reflect light coming from behind you onto the second mirror, which you hold at an angle below the first one. Use this second mirror to reflect the light from behind you a second time so that it enters your eye. Make a diagram to help you explain why the reflected world behind you seems to be upside down.

Repeat the experiment, but this time use the first mirror to reflect light from in front of you onto the second mirror and from there to your eye. Explain why this reflected light produces a world that is right side up.

2.4 Curved Mirrors*

Not all mirrors are plane (flat-surfaced); some have curved surfaces. Those that curve inward, like a saucer, are called concave mirrors. Those that bulge outward, like your eyeball, are said to be convex.

Things you'll need:
- sunglasses
- plane mirror
- convex mirror, if possible
- concave mirror such as a having or makeup mirror
- white cardboard or similar material to make a screen

Convex Mirrors

Many cars and trucks have convex mirrors on the right-hand side of the vehicle. Often trucks and buses have a convex mirror within a larger plane mirror on the driver's side.

Place a pair of sunglasses on a table in a well-lighted room. Look at the front surfaces of the glasses. As you can see, the glasses are convex; they curve outward. Look closely at one of the two lenses. Notice that you can see your image and the images of a number of nearby objects in the glass. Place a small plane mirror beside the glasses. How do the sizes of images seen in a convex mirror compare with the sizes of the same images seen in a plane mirror? Figure 14 shows how an image is formed when light strikes a convex mirror.

If possible, examine the images formed by convex mirrors on the sides of cars or by the large convex mirrors found in stores. Are the images you see in these mirrors smaller than those you would see in a plane mirror? See if you can figure out why large convex mirrors are often found in stores.

Concave Mirrors

Relatively inexpensive concave reflectors are common in shaving and compact or makeup mirrors. Large, expensive, carefully made concave mirrors are found in telescopes such as the one at Mount Palomar, California.

Hold a shaving or makeup mirror close to your face. How does the size of your image compare with the image you would see in a plane mirror?

Now move slowly away from the mirror. What happens to the size of your image? As you continue to move farther from the mirror, you will see your image become blurry. Then, at a greater distance, you will find that your image is upside down. Figure 15-a shows how

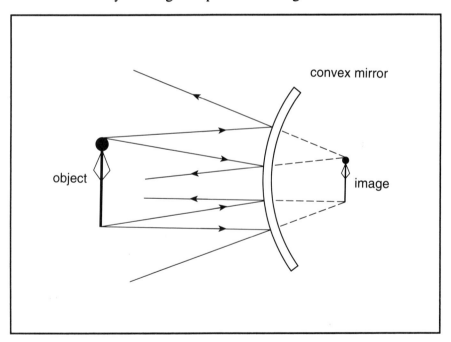

Figure 14) The drawing shows how images are formed by a convex mirror. The lines with arrows represent light rays from the object that are reflected by the mirror. The dotted lines are extensions of the reflected rays to show from where the reflected rays appear to come.

images are formed by reflected light when the object is close to a concave mirror. Figure 15-b shows how images of more distant objects are formed. Notice that the image formed when the object is far from the mirror lies in front of the mirror. Notice, too, that the light rays that form this image actually come back together (converge). The images you have seen before in plane and convex mirrors are called virtual images. These images were located behind the mirrors because that is where the reflected rays appeared to be coming from. In the case of images like the one shown in Figure 15-b, the rays really do meet. That may be why the images that form in front of a concave mirror are called real images.

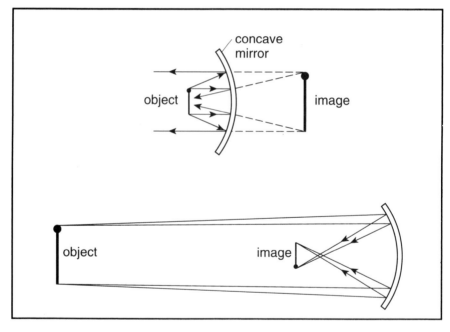

Figure 15) The drawings show how images are formed by a concave mirror. Drawing 15-a shows how the image is formed when the object is close to the mirror. Notice that the image is behind the mirror as it is in a plane (flat) mirror. Drawing 15-b shows how the image is formed when the object is far from the mirror. Notice that this image is in front of the mirror and that the reflected light rays come back together to form the image.

To see that the images of distant objects formed by a concave mirror meet in front of the mirror, try this. Hold the shaving or makeup mirror that you used before on the side of a room opposite a window that looks out onto a bright scene. Have a friend move a sheet of white cardboard, or a similar screen, in front of the mirror. Use the mirror to reflect light coming through the window onto the screen. Move the mirror or screen until you get a clear image of the scene visible through the window. What do you notice about the images? Are they smaller or larger than the objects from which the light came? Are they right side up or inverted?

Models of Concave and Convex Mirrors

Have an adult cut cylindrical surfaces from shiny tin cans. To avoid being cut, **wear gloves.** You can use the shiny metal pieces, about 1.5 in. (4 cm) high and 4 to 6 in. (10 to 15 cm) along the can's circumference, as cylindrical mirrors. (See Figure 16.)

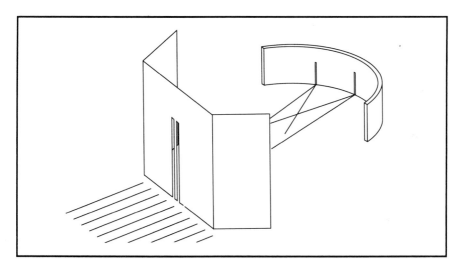

Figure 16) Part of the circumference of a shiny tin can makes a nice model of a curved mirror. What happens to the rays reflected from a concave surface? From a convex surface?

Let light from a distant bulb shine through the two-slit ray maker you used before. Place the concave surface on the two rays as shown in Figure 16. What happens to the reflected rays? How does this model help you explain the real images of distant objects formed by a concave mirror?

Turn the shiny-metal concave cylindrical mirror around to form a convex surface. How does this mirror reflect light rays? Where would the images formed by this mirror be found?

- Find out how reflecting telescopes work. Then use a concave mirror and a small plane mirror to make a model of a reflecting telescope.

- Look at your image in the various mirrors found in a fun house or a house of mirrors at an amusement park or fair. How can you explain the strange images you see in these mirrors? If you have a flexible mirror or some mylar, you can make your own fun-house mirrors.

- In addition to the uses mentioned above, where else do you find concave and convex mirrors? What are they used for?

2.5 Bending the Path of Light*

Place a long pencil in a glass of water. Stand back and look at the pencil through the water. You'll notice that the pencil appears to be broken at the point where it enters the water.

Now hold the pencil so it stands upright in the center of the water. How does the thickness of the pencil that is under water compare with the thickness of the part that is above water?

Use a marking pen to make a small circle near one side of the bottom of a shallow tin can, such as a tuna fish can. Look with one eye straight down onto the small circle as shown in Figure 17-a. Tip the can slightly so the circle just disappears. Have a friend slowly add water to the can while you keep your head steady. As water is added, the circle will reappear.

Place a bright, shiny penny on the bottom of each of two identical glasses. Fill one glass with water. Look down into the glasses to view both pennies at the same time. Which penny appears to be closer?

Things you'll need:

- pencil
- glass of water
- shallow tin can, such as a tuna fish can
- marking pen
- two bright pennies
- two drinking glasses
- white paper
- tape
- black construction paper
- small flashlight and large, clear container, such as a fish tank or slide projector, old 2-in x 2-in slide, and small, clear, rectangular plastic container
- scissors
- pin or small nail
- white file card
- large plastic bag
- solid glass or plastic block or stack of microscope slides
- ruler
- water-filled jar
- white cardboard or other material for screen

All of these strange observations can be explained if you can show that light bends when it passes from air to water. The most direct way to do this is to see if a narrow beam of light bends as it passes from air to water or from water to air. You can do this with a flashlight and a large tank of water, such as a fish tank or a large, clear, plastic container, or with a slide projector and a clear, rectangular, plastic container.

You can make a narrow beam of light by taping a piece of black construction paper over the opening through which light emerges from a small flashlight. Use a large pin or a small nail to make a small hole in the center of the paper. Be sure the hole is directly in front of the bulb's filament so that a bright beam is produced.

Shine the beam along a large, white file card that is partially immersed in water as shown in Figure 18-a. Which way does the beam bend when it enters the water? What do you think will happen if the light passes from water into air?

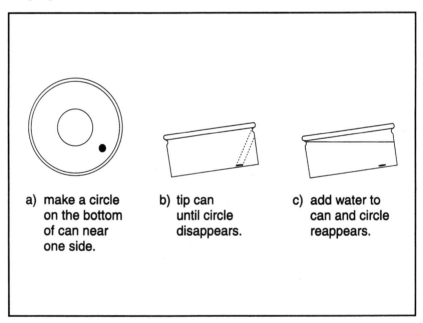

a) make a circle on the bottom of can near one side.

b) tip can until circle disappears.

c) add water to can and circle reappears.

Figure 17-a) Make a small, solid circle on the bottom of a can near one side. 17-b) Tip the can until the circle just disappears. 17-c) Add water to the can, and the circle will reappear.

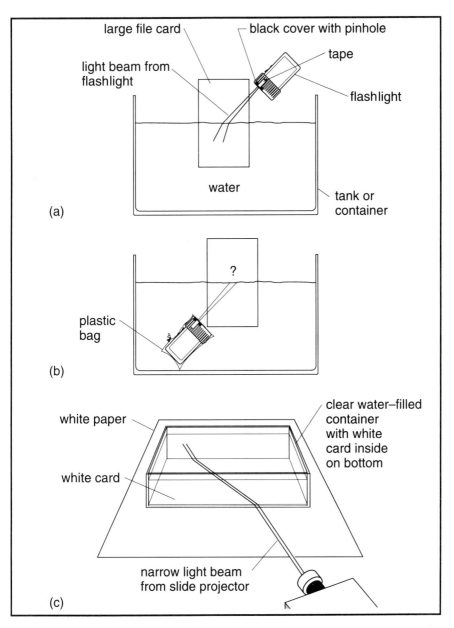

Figure 18-a) How does light bend as it passes from air to water? 18-b) From water to air? 18-c) With a slide projector, the light beam can be seen entering and leaving the water.

To find out, put the flashlight in a plastic bag and seal the bag with a twist-tie. You can then hold the flashlight under water as shown in Figure 18-b. Watch what happens to the beam as it passes from water to air. Which way does it bend?

You can make a single, narrow bright beam with a slide projector. Remove the film from an old 2-in. x 2-in. slide. Replace it with a small piece of black construction paper that has a narrow vertical slit across it. Place this slide in the slide projector. Tip the back of the projector up slightly so that the narrow projected beam can be seen on a sheet of white paper about 12 inches (30 cm) in front of the projector. Focus the projector to obtain a sharp beam.

Cut a piece of white file card so that it fits snugly against the inside bottom of a small, clear, rectangular, water-filled plastic container. Then let the narrow light beam enter the water at an angle as shown in Figure 18-c. The white card on the bottom of the container will allow you to see the light beam inside as well as outside the water-filled container. (You may see another light beam on the surface of the water. You can screen out that beam by covering the upper part of the light beam with your hand.) Does the light bend when it enters the water? When it leaves the water? If possible, repeat the experiment with a solid glass or plastic block. Does glass or plastic bend light?

Another, but less direct, way to do this experiment is to use a plastic or glass block or some glass microscope slides on edge as shown in Figure 19. On one side of the transparent block, use a pencil to draw a straight line at an angle to the glass. The line represents a ray of light coming to the glass. Now look through the other side of the glass and use a ruler to sight along the line you drew earlier. Draw a line along this line of sight. It must be the path the light ray follows on your side of the glass. Extend this line until it meets the glass. Now remove the glass block or slides. What must have been the path of the light inside the glass?

Hold a clear, water-filled jar perpendicular to a beam of sunlight. Ask a friend to hold a sheet of white cardboard behind the jar. Move the jar slowly toward or away from the cardboard until you see a bright line of light on the cardboard. How does this line of light show that light is bent when it passes through the jar of water?

To see if the line of light is due to the water, measure the distance between the jar and the line of light. Then empty the jar and put it back at the same distance from the cardboard. Was it the water that made the light bend?

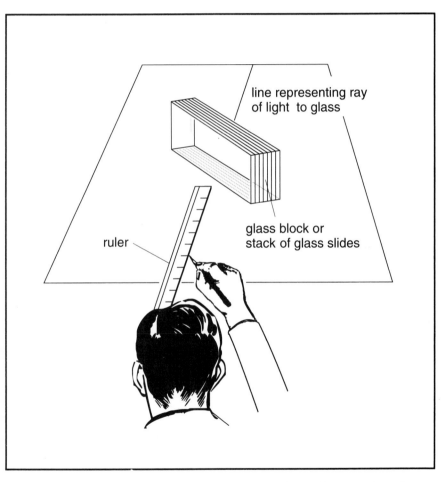

Figure 19) Look through the glass and draw the ray of light as it emerges from the glass block. A ruler will help you establish a line of sight.

49

2.6 Refraction and Lenses*

The bending of light as it passes from air to water, from glass to air, or from any transparent material to a different one is called refraction. You have seen how mirrors, both plane and curved, can be used to produce images by reflecting light from objects. Lenses can produce images too, but lenses make images by refracting light.

Things you'll need:

- hand lens (magnifier)
- glossy page of print
- water
- white cardboard or similar material to make a screen
- round-bottom flask
- fat and thin convex lenses

Lenses that bulge outward, as you would expect, are called convex lenses. Lenses that curve inward at their centers are said to be concave. In this section, you will learn how lenses produce images by refracting light.

You have seen how a cylinder of water can bend a beam of sunlight to form a line of light. If the surface of a clear object is curved in three dimensions; that is, if it is spherical rather than cylindrical, it can be used to form images. A hand lens or magnifier, for example, can be used to make enlarged images of words on a page. Hold a hand lens above the print on this page. Estimate the largest magnification you can obtain with the lens. You can do this by comparing letters that have the same height. Look at one letter through the lens while you view the other letter to one side of the lens. What is the largest magnification you can obtain with the lens?

Lenses and Real Images

Convex lenses can be used to make real images—images that can be seen on a screen—like the ones you made with a concave mirror. To make a real image with a hand lens, hold the lens on the side of a room opposite a window that looks out onto a bright scene. Then move a sheet of white cardboard, or a similar screen, toward or away from the lens until you get a clear image of the scene visible through the window on the screen. What do you notice about the images? Are they smaller or larger than the objects from which the light came? Are they right side up or inverted?

Anything that bends light uniformly can be used to make a real image. Fill a round-bottom flask with water and repeat the experiment you did with the convex lens. You will find that you can make quite good images using the water-filled, round-bottom flask.

Fat and Thin Convex Lenses

Find two convex lenses of different thicknesses; one should be fatter in the middle than the other. Use each lens to make an image of a distant scene through a window as you did before. "Capture" the real images on a screen. Which lens do you have to hold closer to the screen to obtain a clear image? Does the fatter or the thinner lens bend light more? How can you tell?

2.7 A Model of a Convex Lens*

Make two rays of light using the two-slit ray maker you have used before. Or use a slide projector as you did in section 2.5. In place of the slide with a single vertical slit, make one that has two very narrow parallel slits.

Things you'll need:

- two-slit ray maker
- distant light bulb and lamp
- white paper
- clear, flat-bottomed, water-filled cylindrical jar
- small plane mirror

Place the jar of water, which represents a convex lens, on the two narrow beams of light. Is the light bent by the "lens"? Where do the two beams come together?

Now use a plane mirror to deflect one of the rays. The point where the rays meet can be used to represent a point on an "object" just as it did when you examined the images formed in a plane mirror earlier in this chapter. (See Figure 9.) Figure 20 shows the model for a lens. Where is the image of the point of light? Is it a real image? How can you tell?

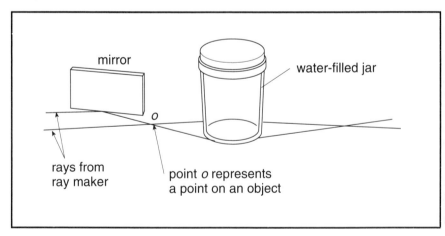

Figure 20) In this model of a convex lens, the jar of water represents the lens. Where is the image of point O?

Figure 21-a shows how a convex lens is used to make enlarged images of objects close to the lens and real images of objects far from the lens. Figure 21-b shows how images are formed by a concave lens. How can you use your water-jar lens and the point on the "object" to make a model of a convex lens that is being used to magnify objects as shown in Figure 21-a(1)?

- Can you make a lens by placing some water in a clear spherical bowl? Can you make a lens using a plastic bag and water?

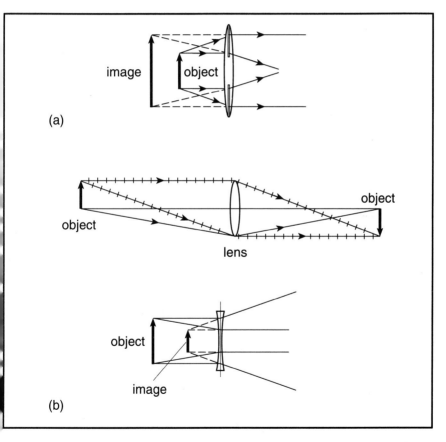

Figure 21-a) Images made by a convex lens 21-a(1) close to the object, and 21-a(2) far from the object. 21-b) An image made by a concave lens.

- Carry out an experiment to find out if the real images made with convex lenses can ever be larger than the objects from which the light comes. You might begin by seeing what effect the distance between the lens and the object has on the size of the image. What do you find?

- Here is a fun experiment that friends and family may find puzzling. Fill two large cylindrical vials or test tubes with water. Add a drop of blue food coloring to one and a drop of yellow food coloring to the other. Securely cap or cork both vessels. On one file card write the word CHOICE in bold capital letters. On a second card write the word MATTER. Place the vial or test tube with the blue water over the card that has the word CHOICE. Place the other tube or vial over the word MATTER.

Can you convince your friends that the yellow lens inverts words while the blue lens does not? Can they demonstrate that it is not because of the color? Can they figure out why one word appears to be inverted and not the other? Can you?

- If possible, examine a concave lens. If you hold the lens near some print, are the images you see larger or smaller than the print? Can you produce real images with such a lens? (See Figure 21-b.)

2.8 Pinholes and Lenses*

In section 1.2, you used pinholes to show that light travels in straight lines. **Ask an adult to help you** set up that experiment again, but this time make three pinholes in the black construction paper. All three holes should be within a half inch (1 centimeter) of each other. Look for the pinhole images on the sheet of white cardboard or paper taped to cardboard. How many images of the candle flame do you see on the cardboard screen? Are they upside down or right side up? How does the size of the images change as you move the screen closer to the pinhole? Farther from the pinhole?

Things you'll need:

- cardboard box
- candle and candle holder
- scissors
- black construction paper
- ruler
- large straight pin, such as a T-pin or hat pin
- dark room
- sheet of white cardboard or sheet of white paper taped to cardboard
- convex lens
- adult helper

Place the screen fairly close to the pinholes so that the images are small but still distinct. Place a convex lens between the pinholes and the images. Can you combine the images by using the lens? See if you can explain what you observe using the lens.

Ask your adult helper to help you repeat the experiment with a new piece of black paper with new pinholes. Make two pinholes, one about twice as wide as the other. How many images do you expect to see? Were you right? What is different about these images? Which pinhole produced the brighter image? How can you tell? Use a convex lens to make a single image. How does the brightness of this image compare with the brightness of the separate pinhole images?

2.9 Refraction in the Atmosphere*

Perhaps you have read stories about people seeing mirages on a desert. They see what appears to be a lake in front of them, but when they get there, they find only more sand. You may have seen mirages. While riding in a car on a hot day, you may notice that the pavement ahead of you looks wet or appears to enter a lake. What you are seeing is not water but an image of the sky. Light from the sky is refracted as it moves through the hot air near the ground. As you can see from Figure 22, the light from the sky that reaches your eye appears to be coming from the ground far away. The refracted blue light from the sky that enters your eyes makes the pavement look wet; it may even look as if the road leads to a large body of water.

Things you'll need:

- slide projector
- light-colored wall
- cardboard
- pin
- hand lens
- tape or a clothespin
- hot plate
- clear, water-filled jar
- aluminum foil
- long, straight wall that faces south
- bright sunshine
- shiny object, such as a key
- level beach with firm, smooth sand

A similar effect is seen in twinkling stars. Such stars are usually close to the horizon, so their light passes through a long stretch of atmosphere before it reaches your eyes. As the atmosphere cools after sunset, air currents are set up. Cool air sinks, and air in contact with the earth's warm surface rises. Starlight coming through this air is bent differently by cool air than by warm air. Since the air temperature through which the light moves changes because of the air currents, the light's path is continually shifting. This shifting of the light from the star makes it appear to twinkle.

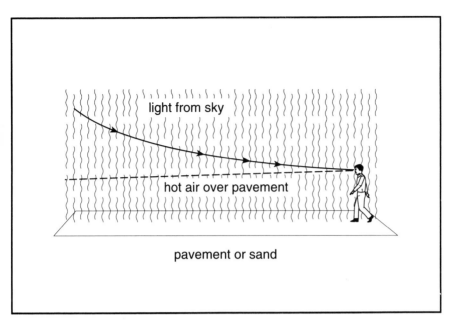

Figure 22) A mirage is created when light from the sky is bent (refracted) by hot air over pavement or sand. To the viewer, the light appears to be coming from the surface far away and looks like water.

Models of Twinkling Star Light

To make light shift as it passes through currents of warm and cold air, place a slide projector so that its light shines on a light-colored wall several meters away. Fix a sheet of cardboard directly in front of the light beam from the slide projector. Make a pinhole in the cardboard so that a small beam of light comes through. Have a friend move a hand lens back and forth between the wall and the pinhole until you have a small patch of light focused on the wall. Move the lens to make the light patch as small as possible. Have your friend hold the lens in that position, so that the small spot of light is fixed and unchanging.

To make air currents, **ask an adult to help you** put a hot plate just below the light beam. When the hot plate is plugged in, the light will have to pass through rising currents of warm air before reaching the wall. What happens to the spot of light on the wall when this happens?

To make another model of twinkling starlight, place a clear, water-filled jar on a crinkled piece of shiny aluminum foil. Do this in a room where the only light is a ceiling light directly over the jar and aluminum foil.

Look down through the water at the aluminum foil. The bright spots of light represent stars. The water represents the earth's atmosphere. Now gently tap the side of the jar with your finger. This will make waves on the surface of the water and change the paths of the light coming from the "stars" to your eyes. In this model, what do the water waves represent?

• If you were an astronaut looking at the stars through the window of a space shuttle high above the atmosphere, why would the stars not appear to twinkle?

Wall Mirages

A small-scale mirage can be produced on an out-of-doors wall. You will need a long, straight wall that faces south so that it is in bright sunshine. This will make the wall warmer than the air beside it. Place your head near one end of the wall. Ask a friend to stand at the other end of the wall and hold a bright shiny object such as a dangling key close to the wall. If the wall is warm enough and long enough (10 meters or more), you should be able to see an image of the key near the wall. As the shiny object is moved closer to the wall, its distorted reflected image appears to approach it also.

On a bright, hot day, you might even find a second image of the shiny object near the wall. Can you find it? If you can, how does it differ from the first image? Can you explain how these images are formed?

Beach Mirages

The beach is a fun place to be on a warm day. It can be even more fun if you look for mirages. To find beach mirages, look for a stretch of level beach that has firm, smooth sand. Place your eye as close to the sand as possible. Then slowly lift your head, just a little. You will notice that you appear to be surrounded by a reflected lake or pond. You may also be able to see the reflected images of objects some distance away that are close to the sand. What do you think makes these images?

3

Light and Color

Normally, we think of light as being white or colorless. But, as you will see, light comes in a variety of colors, which make it even more interesting and beautiful. Nature has provided us with red sunsets, blue skies, green grass, and a variety of colored summer flowers and autumn leaves. The differences in color that we see in a sky at sunset or a landscape at midday must be due to differences in the light coming to our eyes. In fact, you will soon learn that white light can be separated into all the colors of a rainbow. These many colors, in turn, can be combined to make white light.

3.1 Bending White Light to Separate It into Colors*

If you bend light with a prism, as shown in Figure 23-a, it is bent the same way twice. The result is that the light is separated into colors because blue light, for example, is bent more than red light. You can do this by holding a prism in a beam of sunlight. If the sun is shining, you will enjoy changing sunlight into a spectrum of color. **But don't look at the sun!**

Hold your prism so that sunlight streaming through a window can pass through it. Carefully turn the prism until you obtain a bright "rainbow" of colors on the wall or ceiling. How can you tell that the light has been refracted? A less intense rainbow can be obtained by using an electric light bulb as a light source.

Things you'll need:

- glass or plastic prism
- sunlight
- slide projector
- 2-in. x 2-in. slide with vertical slit in black construction paper
- light bulb
- dark room
- white screen or light-colored wall
- drinking glass or small, clear, rectangular plastic container
- flashlight
- white paper

Because the sun keeps changing its position and is sometimes hidden behind a cloud, a more reliable method is to bring the prism to a dark room. There, as you can see from Figure 23-b, you will need a slide projector, the 2-in. x 2-in. slide with a vertical slit in black construction paper that you may have used in section 2.5, a white cardboard screen or a light-colored wall, the glass or plastic prism, and something to support the prism. If you did not make the narrow-slit slide in section 2.5, you can do so by removing the film from an old 2-in. x 2-in. slide and replacing it with a small piece of black construction paper that has a narrow vertical slit in it.

Focus the narrow beam of light on the wall or screen. Then turn the projector roughly 45° from the screen and support the prism in front of the projector. Turn the prism and, if necessary, the projector until you get a bright spectrum of color on the screen. How can you tell that blue light is bent more than red light?

Normally, rainbows are produced when sunlight is refracted and reflected by raindrops. To see a "rainbow" made by passing light

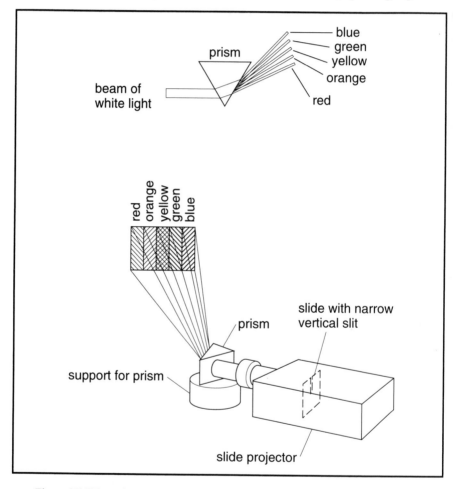

Figure 23) When a beam of white light is refracted by a prism, the colors in the light are separated.

through water, you can use a drinking glass or the small, clear, rectangular plastic container you used before to bend light. Pour water into the glass or rectangular container. Hold the vessel of water above a large sheet of white paper. Let sunlight or a light beam from a flashlight strike the water surface at a sharp angle. You should be able to find a rainbow-like area of colored light beneath the water-filled vessel.

- See if you can make a rainbow the way nature does. Look at the sunlight reflected from a fine spray of water produced by a garden hose. Where do you have to stand to see the rainbow?

3.2 Diffraction: Another Way to Separate White Light into Colors*

Look at the light coming from a clear bulb with a straight-line filament, such as a showcase bulb or the bulb you used in Chapter 1 to make pinhole images and sharp shadows. Be sure the filament is aligned vertically. Then place the single-slit ray maker on a support in front of the bulb so that its opening is directly in front of the filament. This will eliminate unwanted reflections that may be confusing. Look at the filament through a fine-toothed comb or through any narrow slit. You will see the light spread out into bright and dark bands. You may be able to see color in some of the outer bright bands.

Things you'll need:
- clear light bulb with straight-line filament or clear showcase bulb
- single-slit ray maker and support
- fine-toothed comb
- aluminum foil
- pin
- diffraction grating
- slide projector
- old 2-inch x 2-inch slide
- black construction paper
- scissors
- white screen or a light-colored wall
- tape

Use a small pin to make a tiny pinhole in a sheet of aluminum foil. To make an even smaller hole, place the foil on a hard surface and press the tip of the pin against the aluminum. Now look at the light filament through the pinholes. What evidence do you have that light spreads out as it passes through a tiny hole? How does the size of the hole affect the amount that the light spreads out?

As you have seen, light spreads out when it passes through narrow openings or holes. This spreading effect is called diffraction. It is another way to bend light off its usual straight-line path.

Viewing the filament through the tiny openings in a new handkerchief that has been folded once will produce a similar effect, but this time there are many small openings arranged in a regular pattern. An even more dramatic effect can be seen if you look at the filament through a diffraction grating, which has many narrow slits that are very close together. One common diffraction grating has 13,400 slits per inch (5,300 slits per centimeter). You may be able to borrow a diffraction grating from your school or buy one in a hobby store or from a company that sells science supplies. They are not very expensive.

Look at the straight-line filament through the diffraction grating. You may have to turn the grating 90° if the slits are not parallel to the filament. When they are, you will see a bright filament through the center of the grating. To either side of the bright filament, and clearly separated from it, you will see a spectrum—all the colors from violet through red. If you look farther to either side, you may see a second and a third spectrum.

With a slide projector in a dark room, you can capture these spectra on a screen. If you have not done so already, remove the film from an old 2-in. x 2-in. slide. Replace it with a small piece of black construction paper that has a narrow vertical slit in it. Place the projector about half a meter in front of a white screen (a light-colored wall will do). Turn on the projector and focus it until you see a bright vertical slit of light on the screen. Now hold the diffraction grating on the front of the projector lens. You should be able to find a spectra on either side of the bright vertical line of light. If you cannot see the spectra, rotate the grating until the spectra appear. Then tape the grating in place over the lens so you can look closely at the spectra. Which color is diffracted the most by the narrow slits in the grating? Which color is diffracted the least?

3.3 Thin Films: Another Way to Separate White Light into Colors*

You have probably noticed the swirly, multi-colored bands that appear on mud puddles near a highway where oil films float on the water or the colors that can be seen in the surface of a soap bubble. You can easily make some thin films of your own and look for colored light.

Things you'll need:

- pan of water
- clear fingernail polish
- soap bubble solution
- soap bubble ring
- hand lens

Place a pan of water on a kitchen counter. Let a small drop of clear fingernail polish fall onto the water's surface. Now look at the water from different angles until you see the colored light on its surface. Where do you see violet light? Red light? How can you show that the colors are due to light reflected from the nail polish on the surface of the water?

Blow some bubbles using a soap-bubble solution and one of the plastic-handled rings that are found in most bottles of soap-bubble solution. Look closely at the bubbles as they fall in sunlight or a light-filled room. Can you see colors in the surfaces of the bubbles?

Next, dip the plastic ring into the bubble solution, but do not blow into the solution. Instead, hold the ring in front of your eyes with light coming through a window behind you. As the soap drains, it forms a wedge-shaped soap film as shown in Figure 24-a. The film will drain more slowly if you use a cold bubble solution. Look closely at the soap film as it drains. You will see a series of bright-colored bands (Figure 24-b). Each band has all the colors seen in a rainbow. These bands will be easier to see if you view them through a hand lens. In between the colored bands are dark lines. In what part of the film are the colored bands closest together?

As the soap film drains, it becomes very thin at the top. When the film at the top turns black, it means very little light is being reflected from that region of the film. This happens when the thickness of the film becomes thinner than one-quarter the wavelength of light, or about 0.000004 in. (0.00001 cm).

The colors appear because light is reflected from both the front and rear surfaces of the soap film. To explain this phenomenon, you have to assume that light behaves like waves and that different colors have different wavelengths. If the light wave reflected from the second surface is 0.5, 1.5, 2.5, 3.5, etc. wavelengths behind the wave reflected from the front surface, the two waves will match as they leave the thin film. Since the width of the film varies, the wavelengths of some colors

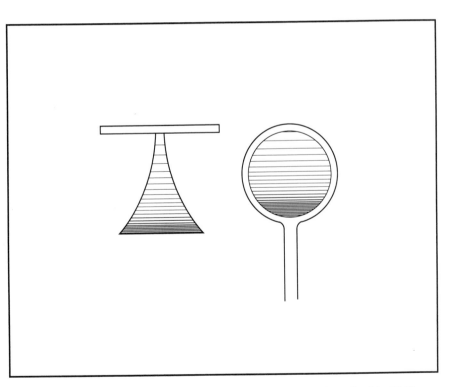

Figure 24-a) As it drains, the soap film forms a wedge, as seen from the side. 24-b) The bands seen in a soap film.

will match at one thickness and those of another color at a different thickness. As a result, the colors are seen at different places along the film. The shorter wavelengths appear higher on the film, where it is thinner, and the longer wavelengths lower, where the film is thicker. The band of colors is repeated each time the thickness of the film increases by a wavelength.

From your observations and the explanation, which color has the shortest wavelength? The longest wavelength?

3.4 Mixing Colored Lights*

Light of different colors can be mixed in a variety of ways. You will find two different ways described here, but there are others. You can choose the one you like best or the one for which you have the right equipment. Perhaps you would like to try both and decide for yourself which one works better. You might even come up with a method that's better than any of the ones described below.

Things you'll need:

- plane mirror
- materials used in previous experiment—diffraction grating, slide projector, old 2-inch x 2-inch slide with vertical slit—*or* three flashlights and red, green, and blue filters
- tape
- white screen (sheets of white cardboard or a white wall)

Mixing Colored Lights Using a Slide Projector, Diffraction Grating, and Mirror

You can use a plane mirror together with the slide projector and diffraction grating that you used in section 3.2 to mix light of different colors as shown in Figure 25. The mirror will allow you to reflect the colors in the spectrum on one side of the bright central beam onto those in the spectrum on the other side. Hold the mirror at a distance from the projector that is about half the distance between the grating and the screen where one of the spectra appear. Reflect the spectrum that is diffracted to one side of the beam so that it lies beside the one on the screen. By carefully turning the mirror you can mix the colors in the two spectra.

The color produced when the blue region of the light in one spectrum overlaps the red region in the other is called magenta. What

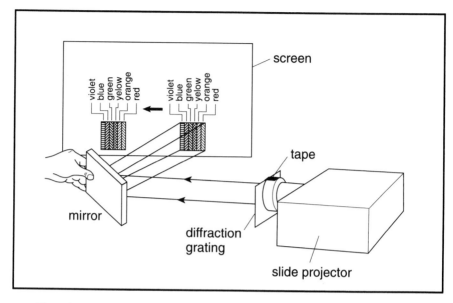

Figure 25) You can mix colored light by reflecting the spectrum diffracted to one side of the diffraction grating onto the spectrum diffracted to the opposite side.

might you have called it? The mixture of blue and green light is called cyan. You might have called it turquoise. A mixture of red and green light, as you can see, is yellow.

Mixing Colored Light with Flashlights

Another way to mix colored lights is to tape red-, green-, and blue-colored filters to three separate flashlights. You can then mix the different colored lights by shining the flashlights on a white screen. Can you make yellow by mixing red and green? Cyan by mixing blue and green? Magenta by mixing blue and red? Can you make white light by mixing all three colored lights?

- The next time you go to a theater to see a play or a musical or watch one that was filmed on a stage, look for colored shadows. See if you can explain why the various colored shadows you see have the colors they do. Are there any you cannot explain?

- Use a hand lens (magnifying glass) to look closely at the screen of a color television. What are the colors of the small rectangles that produce the color? How do they combine these colored squares to produce the colors you see on the screen from normal viewing distance? A weather channel or a channel that provides lots of written messages may be a good one to observe because the picture is not constantly changing.

3.5 Changing Color by Absorbing Light*

When you wear colored or dark glasses, the world does have a different appearance. It may be rosier, bluer, greener, or just darker, but the light passing through the glasses does change the color of the light you see. Colored glass, cellophane, and plastic remove some of the color from white light. The same is true of the pigments and dyes found in food and clothing. A red sweater is red because when white light strikes it, the pigments in the cloth reflect red light and absorb the other colors in white light. Similarly, a green dress reflects the green light that strikes it and absorbs the other colors. What colors do you think are reflected and absorbed by a blue shirt? By

Things you'll need:

- clear plastic containers, such as plastic cups
- food coloring—blue, red, green, yellow
- water
- clear bulb with a straight-line, vertical filament or clear showcase bulb
- diffraction grating
- colored plastic, glass, or cellophane
- single-slit ray maker
- blocks or other supports
- clear plastic vial
- 5-in. x 8-in. white file cards
- white paper
- water color paints and brush

white socks? By black socks? By a magenta blanket? A cyan suit? A yellow coat? In this experiment, you will have an opportunity to check your answers.

When you mixed colored lights, you added one color to another. For example, you added green light to red light to obtain yellow light. The color changes that are brought about by pigments or dyes are done by subtracting or removing colors, not adding them together. You can see this for yourself. Add a few drops of blue food coloring to a clear plastic container, such as a plastic cup. Add water and you have a blue liquid. Now look through the blue liquid to see the white light coming into the room through a window. What is the color of the light after it passes through the blue water? What colors do you think were absorbed by the blue liquid?

Repeat the experiment with red food coloring and water. With green food coloring and water. With yellow food coloring and water. What colors do each of these liquids transmit? What colors do you think they absorb?

Turn on a clear bulb with a straight-line, vertical filament. Look at the bright filament through a diffraction grating. As you know, you will see a complete spectrum if you look to either side of the grating. Now hold a piece of colored plastic, glass, or deep-colored cellophane in front of the grating. Which colors in the spectrum disappear or become dimmer when you do this? Why?

You can check up on your predictions about which colors of light pass through the various colored liquids you made with food coloring. All you need to do is look at the light that comes through the liquids with a diffraction grating. Stand the single-slit ray maker on a block or some other support in front of the showcase bulb or the clear bulb with the straight filament. Then place a clear vial of colored liquid in front of the slit in the ray maker as shown in Figure 26. Be sure all the light passes through the liquid and that you add enough food coloring so that the filament takes on the color of the solution.

Fold 5-in. x 8-in. white file cards to stand on either side of the vial. When you look at the filament through the diffraction grating, you should be able to see the spectrum of colors that come through the liquid on the white paper on either side of the vial. If not, move the cards until the spectrum falls on them.

Which colors are transmitted by the blue food coloring dissolved in water? Which colors are absorbed? If you have trouble seeing exactly which colors are removed by the liquid, have a friend lift the vial so you can see the entire spectrum. Then have him or her slowly lower the vial so you can see which parts of the spectrum are removed or greatly dimmed by the liquid.

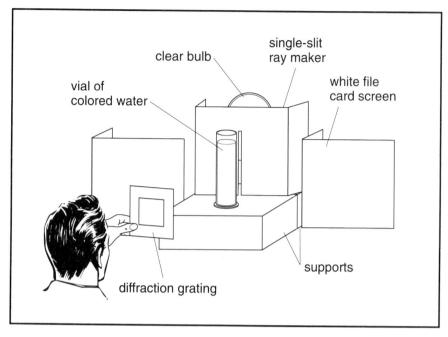

Figure 26) You can use a diffraction grating to find out which colors of light are absorbed and which are transmitted by a colored liquid.

Which colors are removed and which are transmitted by the green liquid? By the red liquid? By the yellow solution of food coloring and water?

Prepare blue, green, red, and yellow liquids in clear plastic containers such as plastic drinking cups. The liquids should be 1 in. (2 to 3 cm) deep. Place a sheet of white paper near a window and look down through each solution. You should be able to see the color that comes up through each liquid clearly. Now look down through two stacked containers; that is, hold the cups, one above the other, and look down through both solutions. From your analysis of the colors transmitted by the solutions using the diffraction grating, can you predict what color you will see when blue is stacked on yellow? Blue on red? Blue on green? How many different two-layered stacks can be made with these four colors? How many three-layered stacks can be made? You may need a helper to make the three-layered stacks and the one four-layered stack.

How closely do your predictions agree with your observations? If you made any wrong predictions, can you explain now where you went wrong?

Try mixing the pigments in different colored paints, such as water colors. What color do you think you will get if you mix blue (cyan) and yellow paint? Blue and other colors? Various combinations? Can you explain the different colors you obtained by mixing paint?

3.6 Color in Colored Light*

Have you ever noticed how cars take on new and different colors in a parking lot illuminated by sodium vapor lamps? The yellow light produced by the lights appears to change the color of cars as well as clothes and skin.

To see how the color of objects is affected by the color of the light in which they are seen, you will need the equipment listed and a dark room. Put the 2-in. x 2-in. slide with the slit in black paper into the projec-

Things you'll need:

• diffraction grating

• slide projector

• tape

• 2-in. x 2-in slide with vertical slit in center of black paper

• white screen

• narrow strips of red, green, blue, cyan, yellow, magenta, white, and black construction paper or yarn

tor and turn on the light. Tape the diffraction grating over the lens so that a bright, vertical line of light and spectra are produced on a screen in front of the projector. Move the screen or projector so that the narrow beam of white light passes on to a distant wall but the spectrum on one side remains clearly visible on the screen.

Place a narrow strip of red construction paper or yarn in the spectrum. What is the apparent color of the paper or yarn when you hold it in the red light of the spectrum? In the blue light? In the green light?

Repeat the experiment with each of the colored paper strips or pieces of yarn. Which colored paper or yarn, as it is moved across the spectrum, takes on every color of the spectrum? Which strip appears black in all parts of the spectrum? Why does the red strip appear to be black in the blue part of the spectrum? Can you explain why the color of some of the strips changes as they are moved slowly across the spectrum?

• Make a rainbow of parallel colored marks on a sheet of white paper using colored pens or crayons. Arrange the colored strips as you would see them in a rainbow—violet, blue, green, yellow, orange, and red. Then look at the colored strips through a piece of deep red glass, cellophane, gelatin, or plastic. Which colors can be seen through the red filter? What do the other colors look like? Repeat the experiment with a green, a blue, and other colored light filters. Which colors can be seen through each filter? What do the other colors look like? How can you explain your results?

- Cut a hole about 1 in. (2 to 3 cm) in diameter in one end of a cardboard box. (A shoe box will do nicely.) Cut a square opening about 3 in. (8 cm) square in the top of the box. Cover the square hole on top with a sheet of red cellophane, gelatin, or plastic. Place a green object and a red object inside the box. You might use balls of colored yarn or red and green apples. Let light from a lamp or flashlight enter the box from above through the colored filter. Look through the hole in the end of the box. What color does each of the objects appear to be when viewed in red light?

Repeat the experiment with a green filter over the square opening. What color does each of the two objects appear to be now? How can you explain the results of these experiments?

Can you predict the results if you added a blue object to the box? If you repeated the experiment with a blue light filter and a blue object in the box? If you repeated the experiment with either a cyan, a magenta, or a yellow filter covering the square opening?

- Look for colored lights that you commonly see. You will find them not only indoors but outside as well. Notice, for example, how the light changes at sunrise or sunset. How does the changing light affect the color of grass, clouds, flowers, trees, houses, and other objects?

- Shine a bright flashlight through the flesh in your fingers or the edges of your hand. What colors are absorbed by your flesh? What colors are transmitted? Why do you think the color of light passing through flesh is changed?

3.7 Blue Sky, Yellow Sun, and Red Sunsets*

Light comes to us from the sun. To reach the earth, the light must first pass through a blanket of air that makes up the miles-thick atmosphere that covers our planet. Like all gases, air is made up of tiny particles. These particles, which are so small that we cannot see

Things you'll need:

- clear drinking glass filled with water
- powdered nondairy creamer
- spoon
- frosted light bulb and lamp

them even with a microscope, are called molecules. The molecules of air, as well as tiny particles of dust in the atmosphere, absorb some of the sunlight that strikes them. These particles then release the "captured" light, not just in the direction the light was going when it was absorbed, but in all directions. Because the light from the particles is sent out in all directions, we say the light is scattered.

The scattering of sunlight by particles in the air has the same effect as many tiny light bulbs emitting light in all directions. Because there are many molecules of air, they fill the sky above us with scattered light. But these molecular lights are *not* tiny suns. The sun emits white light—a mixture of all the colors in the rainbow. But the particles in air are choosy, they scatter lots of blue light and very little red light. As a result, the particles act like zillions of tiny blue bulbs filling the sky with blue light.

The sky is blue only because the particles scatter much more blue light than red light. If the particles in air scattered mostly red light, the sky would appear red.

Molecules of air are far apart—about ten or more times the size of the molecules themselves—but the atmosphere is many miles thick; consequently, sunlight strikes a vast number of molecules before it reaches the earth. You can make an artificial atmosphere that will cause light shining through it to strike many molecules within a short distance. To do this, fill a clear drinking glass with water. The water will serve as the atmosphere. Have a friend hold the glass about a yard (meter) from a bright, frosted light bulb. The light coming through the water-filled glass represents sunlight coming through a very clear atmosphere. Look at the light from the side. Can you see any scattered light? That is, is any of the light traveling through the water scattered to your eyes?

Now look at the color of the "sun" (light bulb), which you can see by looking through the "atmosphere" (water) from the side opposite the bulb. What is the color of the sun seen through this clear atmosphere?

To increase the number of "dust particles" or "molecules" in this atmosphere and thus produce more scattering, just add a small amount of a powdered nondairy creamer. Stir the powder into the water with a spoon. Now look at the atmosphere or sky from the side again. Notice that the color of the "sky," as seen from the side of the glass, has become slightly blue. The scattering of the light has increased. Look again through the atmosphere toward the sun. What is the color of the sun now?

Continue to add more powdered nondairy creamer in small amounts. Check the model sun and sky after each addition. What happens to the color of the sky? To the color of the sun? Can you produce a red "sunset"?

- Sometimes, when the moon rises, it has an orange or bright yellow color rather than its usual pale yellow. What do you think causes this difference in color? Would you expect to see such a moon more frequently during one season than another? If so, when would you think it more likely to occur? Why?

- There is no atmosphere on the moon. Astronauts who have been on the moon reported that the sky over the moon is not blue. It is black! Can you explain why?

3.8 Polarized Waves on a Rope*

You have seen that some properties of light can be explained by assuming that light is wave-like. In fact, many of light's properties can be illustrated by watching water waves or waves moving along a rope.

Things you'll need:

• clothesline or thin rope, about 15–20 feet long

• board with slot about 1 in. (2.5 cm) wide and at least 12 in. (30 cm) long

You have probably noticed that when a water wave passes a fishing bob or cork, the cork simply moves up and down. It does not travel along with the wave. If you dip your finger into a pan of water, you can see the waves move outward from your finger, reflect from the sides of the pan, and move back to your finger. But the particles of water, which give rise to the wave, simply move in a nearly circular fashion as the waves pass. Light waves are believed to behave in a similar fashion; however, the movement of light waves requires no matter. The waves are electromagnetic; they are changing electric and magnetic fields that move through space in the same way as radio, television, radar, and X-ray waves.

We can represent a side view of a light wave with a diagram like the one in Figure 27-a. This looks very much like a water wave, but it does not reveal the fact that a light wave can oscillate (move back and forth) in any direction, not just up and down. Figure 27-b shows an end-on view of a light wave. The arrows show a few of the infinite number of directions that a light wave can oscillate.

Sunlight reflected from water or glass is polarized; that is, the reflected light vibrates mostly along a vertical or a horizontal axis as shown in Figures 27-c and 27-d. The amount of polarization depends on the angle at which the light strikes the reflecting surface.

Light is also polarized by various crystals, including a thin film widely known as Polaroid, which is its trade name. Polaroid transmits light waves that vibrate along only one of the many modes of oscilla-

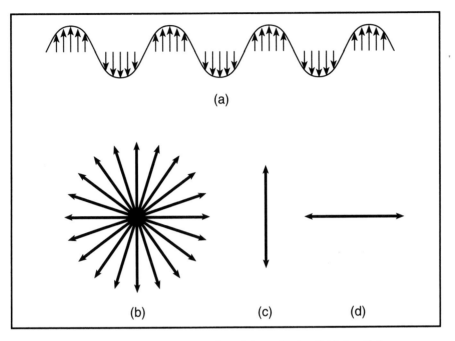

(a)

(b)   (c)   (d)

Figure 27-a) Side view of a representation of the oscillating fields in a light wave. 27-b) End-on view of a representation of a light wave showing the equal likelihood of oscillation in all directions. 27-c) End-on view of oscillation of light waves polarized in the vertical direction. 27-d) End-on view of oscillation of light waves polarized in the horizontal direction.

tion shown in Figure 27-b. The long thin crystals within Polaroid absorb some of the light to form a polarized beam. These crystals act something like the regularly spaced trees in an apple orchard. If you try to run between the rows of trees with a long stick, you can do so only if you hold the stick vertically. Sticks carried horizontally will be stopped. In much the same way, Polaroid allows light waves that oscillate in one direction to be transmitted, while absorbing light that oscillates in the other direction. Figure 28 is an illustration of how Polaroid works.

You can get a better feeling for a light wave by making some waves of your own on a length of old clothesline or thin rope. (Don't try to use new, stiff clothesline.) Ask a friend to hold one end of the

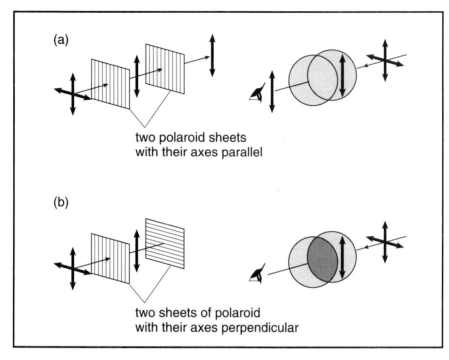

(a)

two polaroid sheets
with their axes parallel

(b)

two sheets of polaroid
with their axes perpendicular

Figure 28-a) If two Polaroid sheets are aligned with their axes parallel as shown, light passing through the filters will be polarized in the vertical direction. 28-b) Light passing through the first Polaroid sheet will be vertically polarized. Very little light will pass through the second sheet because it will absorb waves with vertical oscillations.

rope or tie it to a post. Hold the other end of the rope and stand far enough from your friend so that the rope is off the ground. The rope should be slightly slack so that when you move your hand up and down quickly you can generate waves like the ones shown in Figure 29-a. These waves correspond to light waves that are polarized in the vertical direction. If you move your hand from side to side quickly, you can produce waves that are polarized horizontally (Figure 29-b). If you spin your end of the rope in a small circle with your hand the way you might if someone were jumping rope, you can produce spiral-like waves. (See Figure 29-c.) The number of waves will depend on the length of the rope and how fast you spin it. This is a good model of an unpolarized light wave, which oscillates along all possible axes perpendicular to the motion of the wave itself.

To make a model of what happens when a light wave passes through Polaroid, send unpolarized waves through a picket fence. Or have a friend hold firmly in place a thick sheet of cardboard that has a slot in it as shown in Figure 29-d. How can you use the slot in the cardboard to change the waves shown in Figure 29-c into waves that are polarized vertically? Horizontally? In this experiment, for what does the slotted cardboard serve as a model?

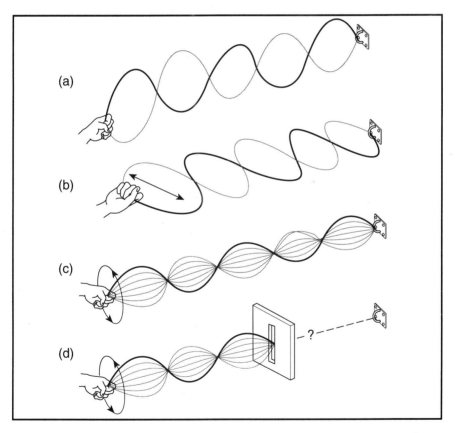

Figure 29-a) A vertically polarized wave. 29-b) A horizontally polarized wave. 29-c) An unpolarized wave oscillates in all directions. 29-d) An unpolarized wave and a polarizer.

3.9 Polarizing Experiments*

Is the scattered light from the sky polarized? To find out, look at some blue sky, about 90° from the sun, through one of the lenses in a pair of Polarized sunglasses or a sheet of Polaroid. Slowly turn the Polarized lens or sheet. Does the intensity of the light change? Does the Polaroid remove more light from the sky when turned one way than another? How can you tell that the sky's scattered blue light is polarized?

Now look through the same piece of Polaroid at a region of the sky below the sun or closer to the sun. **Never look directly at the sun! It can seriously damage your eyes.** Is the light from this part of the sky as polarized as light you viewed previously? How can you tell?

Prepare a glass of water into which you stir a pinch of nondairy powdered creamer. (See section

Things you'll need:

- two pairs of Polarized sunglasses or small Polaroid sheets or disks
- sunlight
- clear drinking glass with water
- nondairy powdered creamer
- spoon
- slide projector
- water
- glass
- glossy book cover
- bowl
- mirror
- bright light bulb
- clear corn syrup
- plastic sandwich baggies
- pieces of plastic
- plastic wrap
- cellophane
- clear cellophane tape

3.7.) Place the glass in the beam of light from a slide projector. Look at the blue light scattered by the particles with a Polaroid lens or sheet in front of your eye. If you rotate the Polaroid, do you think you can change the intensity of the blue light that reaches your eye? Try it! Were you right?

Is all light polarized? To find out, rotate a Polaroid lens or sheet in front of your eye as you look at light from an ordinary frosted light bulb. Is the light from the bulb polarized? Is light from a fluorescent bulb polarized? How about sunlight reflected from the moon?

Polaroid and Glare

Take your Polaroid lens or sheet outside on a sunny day. Find some light reflected from water or glass that produces a glare. Now look at the same light through Polaroid. What happens to the glare as you rotate the Polaroid? Is the glaring light reflected from water or glass polarized? How can you tell?

Place a book with a glossy cover so that it reflects light from a single bright light bulb. Look at the glare from the light bulb that is reflected to your eye by the glossy cover. Place a Polaroid lens or sheet in front of one eye and rotate it slowly. How can you tell that the reflected light is polarized?

If you look closely, you can see that the amount of polarization depends on the angle between the light and the surface. At a particular angle, practically all of the light is polarized. Make an estimate of this angle. Is it about 0°? 30°? 45°? 60°? 75°? 90°?

Repeat the experiment using water in a bowl to reflect the light. Then use a mirror to reflect the light. Is light reflected from water polarized? Is light reflected from a mirror polarized? If it is, does there seem to be a particular angle at which the polarization is a maximum?

Rotating Polarized Light

Some materials rotate polarized light. That is, they turn the plane that is polarized. For example, if you place a sheet of Polaroid in front of a piece of clear cellophane, the cellophane turns the plane of polarization of the light that passes through it. Instead of continuing to oscillate horizontally, the light might rotate 10° to one side of horizontal.

Therefore, to see that light through a second Polaroid, you would have to rotate the second Polaroid 10°.

Since the amount that the polarized light is rotated depends on the wavelength (color) of the light and the thickness of the material, you may see different colors coming through the second Polaroid as you rotate it.

To see the colorful changes that can be produced by rotating polarized light, you will need a jar of clear corn syrup, a good light source, and a pair of Polaroid lenses or sheets. If you have two pairs of polarized sunglasses, put on one pair. If not, hold one Polaroid lens or sheet close to your eye. Place the jar of corn syrup near a bright window, light bulb, or in the beam of a slide projector. Then hold a second Polaroid lens or sheet between the light and the clear syrup. Rotate this Polaroid slowly. What happens to the color that you see through the other Polaroid? Can you explain what is happening?

Try the same experiment with plastic sandwich baggies, pieces of plastic, plastic wrap, cellophane, or clear cellophane tape. Not all clear plastic tapes will rotate polarized light, but generally the inexpensive, yellowish tape is more likely to work. You can also see the effect if you use the plastic support that holds the tape. Once you find such tape, you can criss-cross it in various ways on a plastic sheet. The various thicknesses will rotate the different colors in the polarized light by different amounts so that you can see many colors at the same time by looking through the Polaroid in front of your eye.

- Prepare a collage of materials that rotate polarized light on a clear plastic sheet. Support the sheet above a light source with a Polaroid sheet between the light and the plate. Look at the collage from above through another Polaroid. What do you see? Invite your friends and family to observe your collage. They'll like it!

4

Absorbed Light and Heat

Some objects appear to be red, green, blue, or some other color when viewed in natural light. In Chapter 3, you found that colored objects absorb some of the light that strikes them and reflect the color or mixture of colors that gives them their particular appearance. A yellow object, for example, reflects red and green light and absorbs blue light. Could it be that a black object absorbs most of the light that strikes it? What happens to the light that is absorbed?

In this chapter, you will explore these questions and more. You will also find ways to use sunlight to heat water or air and learn how the color of the clothes you wear can affect your comfort.

4.1 Light, Heat, Black, and White*

To see whether a black object absorbs more light than other colored objects, hold a sheet of black and a sheet of white construction paper in front of a bright light or window. Does less light come through the

Things you'll need:

• sheets of construction paper—black, white, green, red, blue, yellow

• bright light or window

black paper than through the white paper? How about yellow construction paper? Red paper? Blue paper? Green paper?

4.2 What Happens when Light Is Absorbed*

You have seen that black paper absorbs more light than paper of other colors. But what happens to the light that is absorbed? One possibility is that the light is changed to thermal energy; that is, the light absorber becomes warmer—its temperature rises.

To see if this is true, find two identical aluminum pie pans. Pour 3.5 ounces (100 ml) of water into each of them. Add a few drops of black ink to the water in one of the pans—enough to make it impossi-

Things you'll need:

• two identical aluminum pie pans and another aluminum pan that is larger or smaller than the other two

• thermometer

• water

• black ink

• cardboard sheet

• clear plastic wrap

• graduated cylinder or measuring cup

ble to see the bottom of the pan through the dark water. Place the pans side by side on a sheet of cardboard. If the temperature is above freezing (0° C or 32° F), place them in a shady place outdoors until the water in both containers is the same temperature as that of the air.

Then cover both pans with clear plastic wrap and place the pans on the cardboard in bright sunshine. Be sure that the same amount of sunlight falls on both pans.

After an hour or so, measure the temperature of the water in both pans. Has the water in either pan been warmed by the sun? What evidence do you have to support the idea that absorbed light is converted to thermal energy (heat)? What evidence do you have that blackened water absorbs more light than ordinary colorless water?

Repeat the experiment, but this time pour 3.5 oz. (100 ml) of dark water into each pan. Cover one pan with clear plastic wrap; leave the other pan uncovered. Does covering the pan make a difference?

Repeat the experiment once more. This time use a small pan and a large pan—one with a larger diameter. Add ink to 7 oz. (200 ml) of water and pour 3.5 oz. (100 ml) of the darkened water into each pan. Again, cover the pans with clear plastic wrap and place them in bright sunshine as before.

Which pan of water do you think will be warmer after an hour? Or do you think they will have about the same temperature? Measure their temperatures with a thermometer. Were you right? How can you explain your results?

- Here's another way to do this experiment. Find two identical, shiny tin cans. Use flat black paint to cover the surface of one can, or wrap one can in black construction paper. When the paint is dry or the paper in place, add equal amounts of water at the same temperature to both cans. Place the cans on a sheet of cardboard in bright sunshine. Leave them there for several hours. Record the temperature of the water in each can at fifteen-minute intervals. What do you predict the results will be? Were you right?

- Will air enclosed in a black or dark container become warmer than an equal amount of air in a clear container when both receive the same amount of light? Design an experiment of your own to find out. Why should both containers have the same size and weight?

4.3 Light, Heat, and Color*

You have seen that black objects absorb light and that the light is converted to thermal energy (heat). If colored objects absorb some of the white light that strikes them and reflect the rest, then it would be reasonable to expect that colored objects would show an increase in temperature if placed in sunlight. For example, a red ball reflects red light, but if it absorbs the other colors in white light, it should get warmer in sunlight. And it should get warmer than a white ball, which reflects most or all of the light that strikes it.

Things you'll need:

• five or more identical thermometers

• colored sheets of construction paper—black, white, green, red, blue, etc.

• scissors

• clear tape

• cardboard sheet

• sunlight

To see if this is indeed true, you will need a few identical thermometers. You might be able to borrow them from your science teacher if you explain what you want to do. Cut rectangles of identical size, 4 in. x 2 in. (10 cm x 5 cm) is good, from sheets of black, white, red, blue, and green paper. (Include other colors if possible.) Wrap each colored strip around the bulbs of separate thermometers. A small piece of clear tape can be used to keep the paper in place.

Place the thermometers side by side on a sheet of cardboard. Record the temperature of each thermometer just before you put the cardboard in a bright sunny location. Record the temperature inside each colored sheet at two-minute intervals for the next half hour.

Which colored paper would you expect to warm fastest? Which paper does warm fastest? Which paper would you expect to warm the least? Which paper does warm the least? Which paper reflects the most light? The least light?

Make a list of the different colored papers in order of their ability to absorb light.

4.4 Light and Clothing*

Have you ever stood in bright sunlight while wearing a dark shirt, blouse, or sweater? If you have, you may have felt the warmth generated by the light absorbed by the cloth. To see just how much difference the color of the cloth makes in terms of light absorbed, try this experiment.

Things you'll need:

- tape
- two thermometers
- two sheets of cardboard
- pieces of heavy cloth— black, white, and other colors
- clock or watch
- sunlight

Tape two thermometers to the centers of separate sheets of cardboard. Label one sheet "white" and the other "black." Read the temperature on each thermometer and record it. Then tape a piece of heavy, dark cloth over the thermometer on the sheet marked black and a similar piece of white cloth over the other thermometer. Adjust both sheets of cardboard so they are perpendicular to the sunlight. After about half an hour, lift each cloth and record the temperature under each. How much did the temperature change under the black cloth? Under the white cloth? Does the color of the clothes you wear have a significant effect on your comfort?

Repeat the experiment using other heavy pieces of colored cloth. What do you find?

Where might it be advantageous to wear white clothes? Dark clothes? Why do people who live on the desert often wear white clothes? Are polar bears at a disadvantage because they are white?

4.5 Light, Heat, and Different Materials*

Color is not the only thing that determines how much heat a substance can absorb when light is converted to thermal energy. Given equal weights, some materials require more heat to change their temperature by one degree than do others.

In this experiment, you will try to insure that two different substances receive the same amount of light and, therefore, the same

Things you'll need:
- two identical tin cans
- balance
- sand
- water
- two identical thermometers
- cardboard sheet
- black cloth
- sunlight
- clock or watch

amount of heat. To do this, take two identical tin cans. Place one can on a balance and pour 0.5 lb. (or 200 g) of sand into it. Pour an equal weight of water into the other can.

Put a thermometer in each can. If their temperatures are not very nearly the same, leave them in a room until they are. Record the temperature in each can. Then put both cans on a sheet of cardboard. Place the cardboard in a sunny place and cover both cans evenly with a black cloth so the light falling on the cloth will warm both cans.

Record the temperature in each can at ten-minute intervals for at least two hours. Which can warms faster? Which substance, sand or water, requires more heat for its temperature to rise by one degree?

Remove the warmer substance from beneath the black cloth and set it aside until the temperature of the two substances is the same. Then place both cans in a cool place out of the sun. Again, record the temperature in each container at ten-minute intervals for an hour or so. Does water or sand cool faster? Can you explain why?

- Repeat this experiment using water and ordinary soil. Are the results similar?

Water, Sand, Sun, and Wind

If you have ever been at a beach by the ocean or a large lake on a warm day, you may have noticed that by midday there is usually an onshore breeze—a wind that blows from water toward land. The breeze arises because the temperature of the sandy beach and the land behind it rises much more rapidly than does the temperature of the water. Sunlight falls evenly on both land and water, but as you have seen, water must absorb more heat than sand or soil to increase its temperature by one degree. As the air above the warm land is heated, it expands and rises. The cooler, denser air over the water then moves in to replace it, giving rise to the onshore breeze.

At night, the opposite happens. The land cools faster than the water. As its temperature falls below that of the water, the air begins to move from land to water producing an offshore breeze.

The inability of sand to hold large quantities of heat explains why a desert, which is often unbearably hot in the daytime, may become

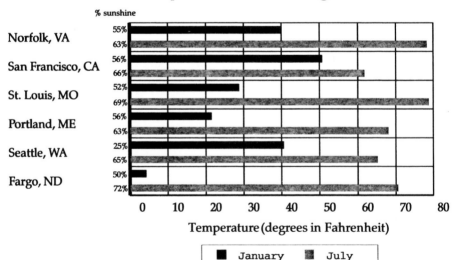

Temperature vs. Sunlight

% sunshine

Norfolk, VA — 55% / 63%
San Francisco, CA — 56% / 66%
St. Louis, MO — 52% / 69%
Portland, ME — 56% / 63%
Seattle, WA — 25% / 65%
Fargo, ND — 50% / 72%

0 10 20 30 40 50 60 70 80

Temperature (degrees in Fahrenheit)

■ January   ▓ July

very cold at night. On the other hand, water's ability to absorb large quantities of heat explains why the temperature of large bodies of water changes very slowly. As a result, temperatures near the ocean do not vary as dramatically from season to season as do temperatures in desert or prairie climates. As you can see from the table on the previous page, the average summer and winter temperatures of cities near an ocean are much closer than those of cities located inland, even though they may receive about the same amount of sunshine.

4.6 A Model Solar Collector*

As energy costs rise and the pollution due to burning fossil fuels increases, more and more thought is given to using the energy in sunlight—a form of energy that costs nothing. You have seen that when light is absorbed it can be converted to heat. You have also seen that water or air can be warmed by sunlight. The effect is enhanced if the space is covered with a clear material and if a dark color is used to absorb the light. These same factors are used in building solar collectors to heat water or air in homes that use energy from the sun.

Things you'll need:
- two cardboard boxes of different sizes, such as a shoe box and a larger box
- masking tape
- thermometer
- clock or watch
- black construction paper
- clear plastic wrap
- newspaper

To make a model solar collector, you will need a cardboard box, such as a shoe box. Remove the top and tape a thermometer to the inside of one of the long sides of the box. Try to keep the thermometer bulb shaded so that it is not in direct sunlight. Place the box in sunlight and turn it so the bottom of the box is nearly perpendicular to the sunlight. How much does the temperature increase inside the box in fifteen minutes?

Repeat the experiment, but this time line the bottom and sides of the box with black construction paper. What effect does the black surface have on the temperature change in the box when it is exposed to sunlight as before?

Repeat the experiment again. This time cover the open, top side of the box with clear plastic wrap. Seal the wrap to the box with tape. Also, tape shut any openings in the box so that air cannot enter or leave. Does covering and sealing the box have any effect on the temperature change inside the box?

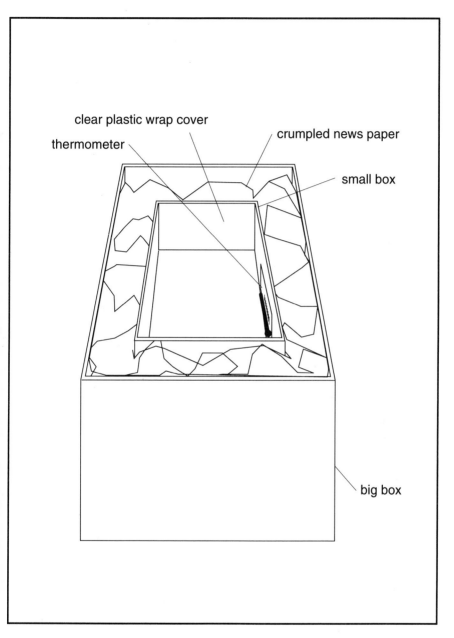

clear plastic wrap cover

thermometer

crumpled news paper

small box

big box

Figure 30) This model solar collector is insulated on five sides by newspaper. Only the top surface is exposed to sunlight, which passes through the clear plastic wrap that is sealed to the box with masking tape.

Finally, repeat the experiment once more. This time put the box inside a larger box that has crumpled newspaper in it. Except for the plastic wrap covering the upper surface, the smaller box should be surrounded by newspaper, which serves as an insulator. (See Figure 30.) What effect does the insulation have on the temperature change inside the box?

If possible, look carefully at a real solar collector. Can you explain why it is built the way it is?

4.7 A Model Solar Home*

In regions where there is plenty of winter sunshine, solar homes are becoming quite common. But solar homes are not a recent invention. Native-American tribes in the Southwestern United States and people elsewhere in the world often built their dwellings with wide entrances that faced south to absorb the warmth of the winter sun. This same principle is used in homes built with large south-facing windows to allow as much light as possible to warm the interiors of the buildings.

Things you'll need:
- cardboard
- scissors
- thermometer
- masking tape
- clock or watch
- black construction paper
- clear plastic wrap

In this experiment, you will build a model solar home and test some of the factors that must be considered in constructing a building that uses sunlight as a source of heat. To begin, you will need some cardboard and a pair of scissors. Cut the cardboard, fold it, and tape it to make a solar house similar to the one shown in Figure 31. The large window in the front will allow sunlight to enter the "building." The window is sloped so that it will be nearly perpendicular to the sunlight. Place a thermometer inside the "house." Its bulb should be shaded and its scale visible through the window. Cover any gaps in the corners or seams of your model house with masking tape.

Take the model outside and place it on a sheet of cardboard to insulate it from the ground. Measure the temperature with the window facing north. Record this starting temperature. Then turn your model home around so that the window is turned directly toward the sun. Record the temperature inside the model home at two-minute intervals, being careful not to let your shadow fall on the model. Continue to record the temperature until it stops rising—a condition called temperature equilibrium, which occurs when heat is being lost from the structure at the same rate it is being produced inside. How long did it take to reach temperature equilibrium? What is the equilibrium temperature? What was the change in temperature inside the house from the time the experiment began until equilibrium was reached?

Line the inside of your model solar home with black construction paper. Then repeat the experiment. How long did it take to reach temperature equilibrium this time? What is the equilibrium temperature? What was the change in temperature inside the house from the time the experiment began until equilibrium was reached? Does lining

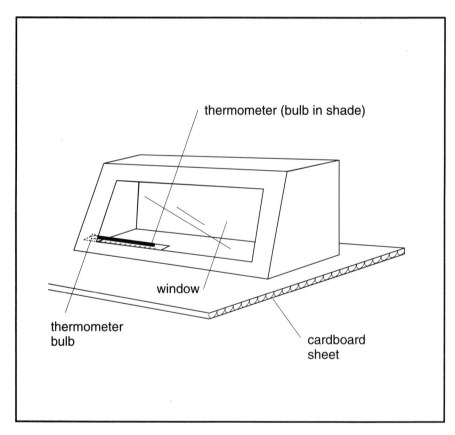

Figure 31) You can build a model solar home like this one from cardboard and masking tape.

the house with black paper make a difference? Does it increase the absorption of light? How do you know?

Repeat the experiment again, but this time cover the window with a piece of clear plastic wrap. Use tape to hold the plastic in place and be sure your plastic window is completely sealed. What is the equilibrium temperature this time? What was the change in temperature inside the house from the time the experiment began until equilibrium was reached? How long did it take to reach temperature equilibrium with the sealed window? Does a sealed window make a difference?

Next, cover the outside of the house with black construction paper. Then repeat the experiment. Does the color of a solar home have any effect on its ability to absorb solar energy?

So far, you have kept the window of your solar home facing the sun. Now try turning the house so the window faces north and repeat the experiment. Repeat the experiment with the house facing east. Then with it facing west. Does the direction that the window faces make a difference? If it could be done, would it make sense to have a solar house turn with the sun?

Finally, place your solar home in a larger cardboard box so you can insulate it. Put crumpled newspapers all around the model between the two boxes as you did with the model solar collector (Figure 30). The model home should be insulated on all sides—floor, roof, and walls—everywhere except over the window. How does insulation affect the equilibrium temperature?

- A solar home may work fine on sunny days, but what happens if there are a few cloudy or stormy days? Obviously, it would be a good idea to store some of the excess solar energy available on bright sunny days so that it is available on cloudy days. See if you can design a model solar home that can store solar energy for inclement weather. You might find what you learned in Section 4.5 useful in your design.

- A solar home painted black inside and out might be a rather depressing place to live. What could be done to increase light absorption in a solar home without painting the entire house black?

- Some solar homes are built into the south side of a hill. Most of the house is buried underground. Only the sun-facing south side is visible. This side is mostly glass with an overhanging roof designed to shade the windows from the high summer sun. Make a model of an underground building and test it. What are some of the advantages of such a home? What are some of the problems? How would you keep such a home cool during the summer?

4.8 Plants and Light*

Without sunlight, life would not exist. The world's green plants are the only living things that can manufacture food, and they depend on light to do it. By a process known as photosynthesis, these plants combine carbon dioxide and water to produce food and oxygen.

Chlorophyll, a green pigment within plant cells, is the catalyst that promotes this chemical change so vital to life. But the energy source for this process is light—usually sunlight. Without light, photosynthesis cannot take place.

To see what happens to plants in the absence of light, lay a small cardboard square or a shingle on some grass. Hold the cardboard or wood in place with a stone or weight. After several days, look underneath. What has happened to the grass? If you detect no change, leave it in place for several more days and check again.

When you have finished the experiment, remove the cover. The grass will slowly recover. How can you tell when it has recovered?

As you found in Sections 4.2, 4.6, and 4.7, a clear cover or window helps convert more sunlight to heat. Because a similar phenomenon is seen in a greenhouse, it is sometimes referred to as the greenhouse effect. The glass or plastic is transparent to sunlight. But when plants and other matter absorb light and become warmer, they emit some of that energy in the form of infrared radiation. Window glass will not allow most of this radiation to pass through it. As a result, much of the energy is trapped and warms the enclosed space just as an infrared heater would.

You can see this effect by covering a small patch of grass with a large glass jar to create your own miniature greenhouse. Watch the grass growing in the greenhouse for several days. How does its rate of growth inside the greenhouse compare with its growth outside?

To obtain as much light as possible, most green plant cells contain growth promoting substances that thrive in the shade. As a result, a plant will grow faster on its shaded side. Why would such a growth pattern make plants turn toward the sun?

To see this effect, put some soil in two small containers. Plant some mustard or corn seeds in both containers. Keep the soil in both containers damp, but not wet, and place them near a window. Cover one set of seeds with a box that has a hole cut in only one side. Leave the other container uncovered. Watch both sets of seeds as they germinate and produce plants. What is different about the way the two sets of seedlings grow? What evidence do you have that plants are attracted to light?

5

Light and Your Eyes

We read books; we watch television; we follow the path of a ball in many of the games we play; we make careful observations as we walk, ride, or experiment. It is obvious that light provides us with an abundance of information. However, before light can provide information, it must enter our eyes where images are formed. But those images convey meaning only if the information encoded within them reaches our brains. Only our brain cells can interpret images; without the active participation of our brains, the images in our eyes have no meaning. Sometimes the images formed in our eyes can cause confusion or lead us to "see" things that are not really there. Depending on conditions, light of certain colors is more useful than others, and sometimes bright lights leave us with long-lasting images that persist even in total darkness. You will explore all this and more in the pages that follow.

Superman and Mistaken Ideas About Vision

The Superman comic strip contained a mistaken concept of vision that is widely accepted. It's an idea that was developed by early Greek philosophers in about 500 B.C. The fictional character Superman was said to have X-ray vision. The drawings showed the X rays coming out of his eyes. Readers did not seem to be concerned that Superman's eyes were the source of the X rays that enabled him to see through concrete walls. Did these readers believe people normally see by radiating light from their eyes and, therefore, saw nothing unusual about Superman releasing a more energetic form of light from his eyes? Or did they simply think that Superman, a creature from another planet, was of a different species with an extraordinary, superhuman capacity for seeing by generating his own light in the form of X rays?

- The idea that humans see by emitting light from their eyes is not uncommon even though it is easily disproven. Design an experiment of your own to show that humans, including yourself, do not see by radiating light from their eyes.

Your Eye

While your eyes are prominently displayed on the front of your face, you see only a small portion of the eyeball and very little of what is inside it. Figure 32 is a diagram showing what is inside the eye. You will notice that the eyeball is almost a sphere with a little bulge at the front. The white part of the eye, some of which is visible, is the rigid sclera, which gives the eye its firm shape. The choroid coat is a black layer of cells that lines the inside of the eye. It absorbs stray light and reduces reflections inside the eye.

The bulge at the front of the eye is the transparent cornea. Light entering the eye is refracted by the cornea before it passes through the round, black pupil, which is simply a small hole in the iris. The pigment in the iris gives an eye its characteristic color. The more pigment, the darker the iris. Light that passes through the pupil enters the transparent, crystalline lens, which refracts the light again. This refraction brings the light rays together to form an image on the eye's retina at the inner, rear side of the eyeball. The space in front of the lens is filled with a fluid called the vitreous humor. The space behind the lens is filled with the aqueous humor. These fluids fill the eyeball and prevent it from collapsing.

Unlike the lenses you have used before, the lens in your eye can change its shape. When you look at objects close to your eyes, the lens becomes fatter. As you saw in section 2.6, a fat lens causes light to bend more. By making your own lens fatter, a process that your nervous system does automatically, diverging light from nearby objects can be brought together (focused) on your retina. When you look at distant objects, your lens becomes thinner. Since light rays coming from distant objects are almost parallel, they do not have to be bent as

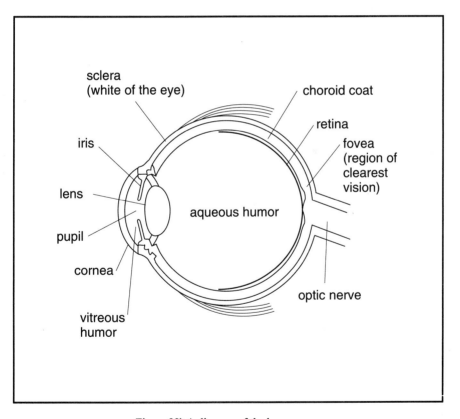

Figure 32) A diagram of the human eye.

much. A thinner lens bends light less so that the rays still come together on the retina.

The retina, which lies on the rear, inside surface of the eye, is rich in nerve cells that are stimulated by light. The light in images formed on the retina stimulates these cells. These cells, in turn, give rise to nerve impulses that travel along the optic nerve to the brain where they may take on meaning.

5.1 A Model of Your Eye*

To make a simple model of your eye (Figure 33), you'll need a spherical, or nearly spherical, glass bowl, such as a small fish bowl, or a glass, such as a brandy glass. When the bowl or glass is filled with water, it will serve as a combination of the cornea, lens, aqueous humor, and vitreous humor. A sheet of black construction paper with a small hole through it serves as the iris when placed in front of the bowl. The hole should be about as high as the center of the water-filled sphere. A sheet of white cardboard, or white paper taped to cardboard, can represent the retina.

Things you'll need:

• spherical, or nearly spherical, glass bowl or glass, such as a small fish bowl or a brandy glass

• water

• black construction paper

• white cardboard sheet or cardboard with white paper taped to it

• clear light bulb with a crescent-shaped filament

A clear light bulb with a crescent-shaped filament can be used as a light source. It should be placed a few centimeters in front of the "iris" as shown in Figure 33. Move the "retina" closer or farther from the sphere-shaped lens until you can see a clear, sharp image. What do you notice about the image? Is it right side up or upside down? Is it reversed right for left?

Retinal Images

People have always found it difficult to believe that the images on our retinas are upside down, but as you found in the previous experiment, they are—or at least the evidence you have collected would strongly suggest that they are. Photographs of the eye's interior have confirmed that the images really are inverted. But even before photography, René Descartes (1596–1650) obtained the eye of an ox that had been slaughtered. When he looked through an opening cut in the back of the ox's eye, he saw the inverted image produced by the eye's cornea and lens.

Of course, we see the world right side up. Somehow, from our earliest days, our brains enabled us to cope with visual images that were upside down. In fact, experiments have shown that right-side-up images on the retina make the world appear upside down. Experiments have been conducted in which people wore special prisms over their eyes so that the images formed on their retinas would be right side up. These people found that their world was suddenly inverted—everything appeared to be upside down. After awhile, however, they learned to cope with their inverted world. With time, they again saw the world as right side up. What do you think happened when they took the prisms off?

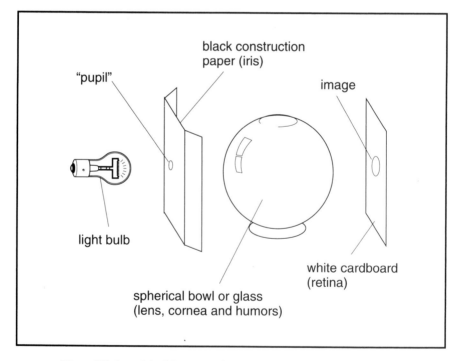

Figure 33) A model of the eye can be made from very common materials.

The Blind spot

In Figure 32, notice the small area of the retina where the sensitive nerve fibers join together to form the optic nerve that leads to the back of the brain. In this region, which is called the blind spot, there are no nerve cells that respond to light. What will happen if an image forms on that part of your eye?

To find out, look closely at Figure 34. It shows a baseball player waiting for a ball that is approaching from the right. Hold the book in front of your face at reading distance. Shut your left eye, stare at the ball player's belt buckle with your other eye, and slowly move the book closer and closer to your open right eye. Can you find a point where the ball disappears? If you can, can you explain why it disappears?

Repeat the experiment with your left eye open and your right eye closed. But this time stare at the ball as you move the book closer to your eye. Can you find a point where the player's belt buckle disappears? Can you explain why? Why might a batter, even with eyes wide open, momentarily lose sight of an approaching pitch?

Seeing Colored Images

Our retinas have two types of cells that respond to light. Rod cells, so named because of their shape, respond to any color, but the color of the light cannot be determined. These cells, which are located around the edges of the retina, respond to very weak light. It is the rod cells of our retinas that enable us to see in dim light.

Cone cells, which are located near the center of the retina directly behind the lens, can detect different colors. These cells, which are not stimulated by dim light, are most concentrated in the area of the fovea (see Figure 32). According to one theory of vision, there are three types of cone cells, one for each of the primary colors of light—red, green, and blue. If light from a blue object enters our eyes, it is mostly the cone cells responsive to blue light that are stimulated. Similarly,

Figure 34) Keeping your eye on the ball does not always work.

green light stimulates primarily the cone cells sensitive to green light, and red light stimulates cone cells that respond to red light. The theory holds that yellow light will excite both the red- and green-sensitive cone cells. Which cone cells would be stimulated by a magenta-colored object according to this theory? Which cells would respond to cyan?

Cone cells lose their sensitivity (their ability to respond to light) quite quickly. As a result, your eyes tend to move back and forth slightly so that new cone cells are stimulated and the ones that are "tired" can rest for a moment and regain their sensitivity.

• Some people are said to be color-blind. Does this mean they cannot see any color? Or does it mean something else? Carry out your own research on color blindness. Then see if you can design a test that will detect color blindness.

5.2 Stop on Red*

Is there any scientific basis for covering brake-indicator lights on cars and trucks with red glass or plastic? Or is it just a matter of convention? It is probably convention. Red has been a sign of danger or a signal to stop for many years. However, there is also a scientific basis, even if accidental, for making brake lights red.

As you know, a fat lens bends light more than a thin one, and the lens inside your eye becomes fatter when you look at objects that are

Things you'll need:

• white paper

• pencil

• ruler

• two-slit ray maker

• flat-bottomed jar like the one you used in section 2.7.

• sheet of white paper

• light bulb

• colored cellophane, glass, plastic, or gelatin—red and blue

nearby. It becomes thinner when you look at distant objects. Light rays reaching your eye from afar are almost parallel when they enter your eye. To see why, draw a small circle at one end of a sheet of paper. The circle represents the pupil in your iris through which light enters your eye.

Place a dot at the other end of the paper. Now draw lines from the dot to the outer edges of the circle. The lines represent light rays coming from the dot to the eye. Repeat the process with a dot that is close to the circle. In which case are the "rays" closer to being parallel?

Imagine a dot that is a room's length from the circle. Would the rays coming from the dot to the edges of the circle be nearly parallel?

Now, look at how a convex lens brings colored light rays to focus. To do so, place a two-slit ray maker in front of a flat-bottomed jar like the one you used in section 2.7. The jar should rest near one end of a sheet of white paper. Use a light bulb on the opposite side of the room as a light source for the rays. (See Figure 35.) Consider the point where the rays meet as the place where light rays would meet on the retina of your eye.

To obtain blue rays, place a thick piece of blue cellophane, a blue glass plate, or a blue plastic or gelatin filter in front of the ray maker or the lens. Carefully mark the point where the blue rays cross (come together) on the paper.

Without moving the paper, ray maker, or lens, repeat the experiment using red cellophane, glass, plastic, or gelatin to produce a pair of red rays. Mark the point where the red rays cross. Is this point slightly closer to, slightly farther from, or at the exact same place that the blue rays crossed? How is this experiment related to the one you did with a prism in section 3.1? Which color in white light was bent

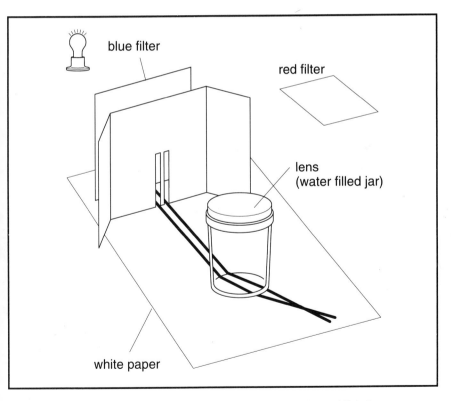

Figure 35) Does a lens bend blue light differently than red light?

most by a prism? Which color was bent least? Is red or blue light bent most by a lens?

As your experiments have demonstrated, red light is not refracted as much as blue light by a lens or prism. To bring red light to focus on your retina, the muscles of your eye have to make your lens fatter. Remember, your lens gets fatter when you look at things that are close to you. Only the thicker lens can bend the light enough to bring the rays together on the retina. So when you look at red light, your brain interprets this response to mean that you are looking at an object that is closer than it really is. Thus, a red brake light appears to suddenly "jump" at you!

Similarly, our brain interprets blue objects as being farther away than they actually are. When you look at a blue sweater, your lens becomes thinner (less convex) in order to bend the rays less and bring them together on the retina instead of in front of it.

Artists make use of this effect in their work. Blue sky, mountains, or seas are used to give depth to a painting. An observer's lens becomes thinner when viewing blue objects. Their brains automatically think, "Aha! the lens is getting thinner, so the object is farther away." Artists use reds, oranges, and yellows to make things stand out or "come forward" in a painting. Viewers see these warm-colored objects as being closer than they actually are. Their lenses have to thicken slightly to bring these colors to focus on their retinas, and their brains interpret the thicker lens to mean the objects are closer.

- Use paints, crayons, or colored pencils to produce a picture that appears to have depth.

- Magazines often use color in their headings to make the words appear to be within or above the page. See if you can find a magazine where this effect is evident. How do these printed words manage to convey a sense of depth?

5.3 Afterimages*

Have you ever looked at a bright light, turned your head away from the light, and continued to see a bright spot no matter where you looked? If not, or to refresh your memory, stare at a bright frosted bulb for a few seconds without moving your head or shifting your eyes. Then turn away from the

Things you'll need:
- bright, frosted light bulb
- light-colored wall
- white pad or file card
- colored filters—red, green, blue, and, if possible, yellow, cyan, and magenta

bright light and look at a light-colored wall. Notice the bright light, rightly called an afterimage, that you see on the wall. What is the initial color of the image? What happens to the color of the image as you watch it? Is the afterimage still present if you close your eyes? For how long does the afterimage persist?

Repeat the experiment, but this time hold a white pad or card in your hand. Once you see the afterimage on the wall, shift your gaze to the nearby card. What happens to the size of the afterimage? Try to explain why the size of the afterimage changes.

Allow time for your eye to recover and the afterimage to disappear. Then stand closer to the bright bulb and look at it again with only one eye open. Keep your other eye closed and cover it with your hand. Can you see an afterimage with the eye that was open? Can you see an afterimage with the eye that was closed? How does this experiment help you decide whether afterimages arise in the eye or the brain?

After resting your eyes again, look at the bright light through a green filter that you hold in front of one eye. Keep the other eye closed. After staring at the bulb for thirty seconds, again turn away from the light and look for an afterimage on the wall. What is the color of this afterimage? Is there a rim of a different color surrounding the afterimage? If there is, what is the color of the rim? Does the color of the afterimage change with time? Is the afterimage present when you close your eye? Is it present in the eye that you kept closed? Try to explain your observations.

Repeat the experiment using a red filter. Then try a blue filter. If possible, use yellow, cyan, and magenta filters to produce afterimages. Can you explain the colors of the afterimages you see?

• Stare at the black ghost in Figure 36 for about half a minute. Then shift your gaze to the center of the haunted house in the same figure. Why do you see a white ghost in front of the house?

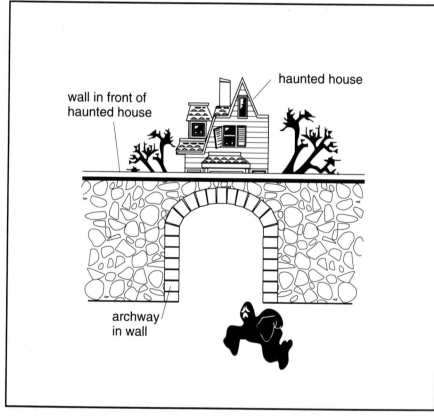

Figure 36) Can you put the black ghost into the haunted house? Could afterimages explain the ghosts that some people claim to have seen?

5.4 Illusions*

Your experiments with mirages showed you that the world is not always as it appears. Illusions lead one to the same conclusion.

Things you'll need:
• ruler
• paper
• pencil
• drawing compass

With paper, pencil, and ruler you can make some illusions of your own. To begin, use a ruler to draw two horizontal straight lines, one above the other. Make both lines exactly 1.5 in. (4 cm) long, and draw them about 0.75 in. (2 cm) apart. At each end of one line draw V-shaped arrowheads. The tips of the Vs should just touch the ends of the line. At the ends of the other line draw similar Vs but turn them around so they look like the tails of arrows. You now have one arrow with two heads and a second arrow with two tails. Which of the lines appears to be longer? Is it really longer?

Draw another line 1.5 in. (4 cm) long. Make a round dot thicker than the line at the exact center of the line. Add a V-shaped arrowhead at one end of the line and a V-shaped arrow tail at the other end of the line. Does the dot still appear to be at the center of the line?

Use the ruler again to draw two vertical, parallel lines on a sheet of paper. Make each line about 3 in. (8 cm) long and separate them by about 0.5 in. (1.5 cm). Mark a point midway between the lines and 1.5 in. (4 cm) from either end. Then draw straight lines radiating outward from this point like the spokes of a wheel. Be sure the lines extend several centimeters beyond both sides of the parallel lines. One line should be perpendicular to the two parallel lines and the others should be at varying angles, about 10° apart, like the lines on a compass.

After you have done this, look at the parallel lines again. Do they still appear to be parallel? What do you think has happened?

Draw a horizontal line about 6 in. (15 cm) long at the bottom of a white sheet of paper. At the line's midpoint, draw a 6in. (15 cm) vertical line perpendicular to the horizontal line. Stand back and look at the lines. Which line appears to be longer? How much of the longer line must you erase before both lines appear to have the same length?

Use a drawing compass to draw a circle that has a radius of about 1 in. (2.54 cm). Then, at about 10° intervals, draw a series of diameters (about eighteen of them) across the circle. Within one quadrant of the divided circle you have made, draw a second circle with a diameter about one-third as large as the first one. Now look at the second circle within the first one. Does it appear to be a perfect circle?

Use the same compass to draw a series of concentric circles as close together as you can make them. The largest might have a diameter of 2 or 3 in. (5 or 6 cm); the diameter of the smallest should be 0.2 in. (0.5 cm) or less. Then draw a square whose center is the center of all the circles. Make the sides of the square about half the diameter of the circle. Stand back and look at the square you have drawn. Does it look like a square?

• See if you can design and draw some line illusions of your own.

5.5 Eyes, Mind, Color, and Concentration*

Colored light, which stimulates the cone cells in your eye, can sometimes have an unexpected effect on your mind. To see that this is true, write the words below on a sheet of paper in the vertical order shown.

Things you'll need:

• white paper

• colored pens or pencils—red, green, blue, and yellow

But use different colored pencils or pens to write the words in thick-lined letters. The colors to be used in writing each word are given in parentheses beside the word.

> red (write letters in blue)
> yellow (write letters in green)
> green (write letters in red)
> blue (write letters in yellow)
> red (write letters in green)
> blue (write letters in red)
> yellow (write letters in blue)
> green (write letters in red)
> blue (write letters in yellow)
> red (write letters in blue)

Read the words from top to bottom and then from bottom to top.

You probably found that quite easy to do, but now try this. Look at each word and name the color of the letters used to write it. Again start at the top and go to the bottom and then back to the top. Not as easy, is it? What seems to be the problem?

Try this experiment on other people. Can you find anyone who can do this with ease?

Bibliography

Beller, Joel. *So You Want to Do a Science Project.* New York: Arco, 1982.

Brown, Bob. *More Science For You—112 Illustrated Experiments.* Blue Ridge Summit, Penn.: Tab Books, 1988.

Gardner, Robert. *Crime Lab 101.* New York: Walker, 1992.

———. *Experimenting with Light.* New York: Watts, 1991.

———. *Ideas for Science Projects.* New York: Watts, 1986.

———. *Investigate and Discover Light.* New York: Messner, 1991.

———. *More Ideas for Science Projects.* New York: Watts, 1989.

Gardner, R., and D. Webster. *Shadow Science.* New York: Doubleday, 1976.

Loiry, William S. *Winning with Science.* Sarasota, Fla.: Loiry Publishing, 1983.

Tocci, Salvatore. *How To Do a Science Fair Project.* New York: Watts, 1986.

VanCleave, Janice. *Astronomy for Every Kid: 101 Easy Experiments that. Really Work.* New York: Wiley, 1991.

———. *Physics for Every Kid: 101 Easy Experiments that Really Work.* New York: Wiley, 1991.

Van Deman, B.A., and E. McDonald. *Nuts and Bolts: A Matter of Fact Guide to Science Fair Projects.* Harwood Heights, Ill.: Science Man Press, 1980.

Walpole, Brenda. *175 Science Experiments To Amuse and Amaze Your Friends.* New York: Random House, 1988.

Webster, David. *How To Do a Science Project.* New York: Watts, 1974.

———. *Photo Fun: An Idea Book for Shutterbugs.* New York: Watts, 1973.

———. *More Brain Boosters.* New York: Doubleday, 1975.

Index

About the Author

Robert Gardner is a retired high school teacher of physics, chemistry and physical science. He has taught in a number of National Science Foundation teachers' institutes and is an award-winning author of science books for young people.